African Pygmy Hedgehogs and Hedgehogs

Hedgehogs as pets: facts and information.

Care, breeding, cages, owning, house, homes, food, feeding, hibernation, habitat, all covered.

Elliott Lang

African Pygmy Hedgehogs and Hedgehogs

Hedgehogs as pets:
Facts and Information

by

Elliott Lang

Published by IMB Publishing

With thanks to my dad for teaching me all about African Pygmy Hedgehogs and Hedgehogs.

Also thanks to my wife and kids for sticking with me throughout the many hours I spent writing this book

Table of Contents

Table of Contents

Table of Contents

Chapter One: Introduction

Hedgehogs. Everyone loves a hedgehog, and what is there to not like? They are cute; with their little noses always twitching and the way that they prance around on their little feet. The only thing that really deters people from warming up to this enchanting pet is the quills.

In fact, the prickly quills protruding from the hedgehog's back make people believe that these friendly little creatures are far from friendly. Thankfully, this is something that the hedgehog is happy to dispel and more and more people are experiencing the joy of owning a hedgehog.

And that is what this book is all about. The joys of owning a hedgehog. Yes, there is work, which I cover in the pages on basic care, health care and socialization, but there are a hundred other things that make owning a hedgehog a rewarding experience.

It is a unique experience and while hedgehogs are often labelled as cage pets, the hedgehog can be a very adaptable pet. They can be housetrained and will enjoy simply playing and cuddling with their owner. In addition, the pets are quite social when they are properly handled and many will adapt very well to travelling.

Although this book is designed to look specifically at the African Pygmy Hedgehog, in the day-to-day care, there are

many similarities and needs shared between all of the different kinds of hedgehogs, which I touch on briefly.
As you can see, there is no limit to the amount of positives that can be said about hedgehogs. This book goes over everything you need to know about raising them, caring for them and even breeding them.

So sit back...hopefully with a prickly friend in your lap...and enjoy this wonderful resource.

Chapter Two: Understanding Hedgehogs

Before you branch out into the world of hedgehogs, it is very important that you understand the hedgehogs themselves. African Pygmy Hedgehogs, as well as other types of hedgehogs, are not an ideal pet for everyone.

Each hedgehog has specific requirements and while they do reside in a cage, they are not a pet that you can simply forget. This is an animal that needs daily care and contact and they can be surprisingly time consuming.

But before we get into their daily care, let's take the time in this chapter to really understand what a hedgehog really is.

What is a Hedgehog

What is a hedgehog? If you have seen them even once, you probably have some idea of what a hedgehog is. They are well known for their small size and the quills that protrude from their back.

Although many people group them together with the rodent family, hedgehogs actually belong to the mammal family called the Erinaceinae. This is a family of shrew, like mammals, that can be found in Europe, New Zealand, Asia and Africa. The Hedgehog itself can be found in all of those locations, however, there is no living species in North or South America and there are no native species in Australia.

Hedgehogs themselves are a nocturnal animal that live primarily on their own. They are rarely seen with other hedgehogs unless they are a nursing mother or are mating.

Hedgehogs live in burrows and they are primarily feed off of insects, making them an insectivore.

In fact, the hedgehog is one of the oldest insectivores that exists today and they have been linked back to over 15 million years. In fact, fossils of hedgehogs from the Neogene Period, which was a period in the earth's history dating from 23.3 million years to 5 million years ago, show that there are no significant changes in hedgehogs throughout history.

The hedgehog is amongst one of the earliest examples of a placental mammal. While hedgehogs have been around for millions of years, the name hedgehog can be traced back to the mid 1400's. The name is derived from Middle English and comes from the words heyg, which means hedgerows and hoge, which describes the pig-like snout that hedgehogs have.

Today, hedgehogs are still a wild animal and thrive in much of its natural habitat. There are 14 species of hedgehog and many of them have made their way into the world of small animal companions. They live extremely well as a pet and can be domesticated very quickly.

Although hedgehogs do have quills, they are not related to the porcupine and their quills are actually quite different from those of the porcupine, which I will go over later in this book.

Types of Hedgehogs

As I have mentioned already, there are 14 species of hedgehogs and while this book does focus on the care for the African Pygmy Hedgehog, it is important to look at the different types of hedgehogs that you can purchase. Remember that when you are buying a hedgehog that you make sure it is the species of hedgehog that you desire.

African Pygmy Hedgehog: The more commonly known hedgehog is the African Pygmy Hedgehog, which this book primarily focuses on. There are many different colours, which I will go over later. The African Pygmy Hedgehog is a domesticated variety of either the 4-Toed Hedgehog or the Algerian Hedgehog.

Algerian Hedgehog: The Algerian Hedgehog is native to North Africa but the small animal has made its way to southern France, southern Spain, Malta, Canary Islands and Djerba. It is between 8 to 14 inches in length and usually weighs between 400 to 1000 grams. The average lifespan for the Algerian Hedgehog is roughly 4 years. In colouring, they usually have a white belly and should have cream and chocolate brown banded quills.

Brandt's Hedgehog: Found in Iran, Afghanistan, Yemen, Pakistan and Oman, this is a medium sized hedgehog that thrives in desert locations. They are usually 9 to 12 inches in length and weigh between 500 to 900 grams. The Brandt's Hedgehog is dark brown in colouring and it has a very long quill that is different to other hedgehogs. The average lifespan is 5 years.

Chinese Hedgehog: Native to Asia, the Chinese Hedgehog can be found in China, Korea and Manchuria. They are usually 12 to 15 inches in length and weight 700 to 1000 grams. The Chinese Hedgehog has chocolate brown banded quills and a brown belly; however, there are variations of colour in this species. They have an average lifespan of 5 years.

Daurian Hedgehog: A long eared variety of hedgehog, the Daurian Hedgehog is native to Manchuria and Eastern Mongolia. They are usually 8 to 11 inches in length and 450 to 700 grams in weight. The Daurian Hedgehog is identified by the brown colouring and the longer ears. They usually have a lifespan of 4 to 5 years.

Eastern European Hedgehog: Native to Czechoslovakia, the Eastern European Hedgehog is normally 12 to 15 inches in length and usually weighs between 700 to 1000 grams. They  are very similar in colouring to the Western European Hedgehog with chocolate brown, banded quills and brown belly but they should have a distinct white patch on their chest. The lifespan of the Eastern European Hedgehog is also about 5 years.

Ethiopian Hedgehog: The Ethiopian Hedgehog is a striking little hedgehog with pale brown quills and a mottled belly of brown, black and white in varying mixtures. There is usually a well-defined dark mask, dark brown legs and a white stripe on the forehead. The length is usually between 6 to 10 inches and the weight between 400 to 700 grams. The average lifespan is 5 years.

4-Toed Hedgehog: This hedgehog is an African species of hedgehog that is native to Central Africa. It is a smaller hedgehog that usually ranges in length from 7 to 10 inches and weight from 300 to 700 grams. The quills are usually banded with chocolate brown and black and the underbelly fur of the 4-toed Hedgehog is white. The lifespan of the 4 toed Hedgehog is usually between 3 to 5 years. One thing of note is the 4-Toed Hedgehog is missing the big toe that is common in all other hedgehog species.

Hardwicke's Hedgehog: Found in Northern India and Eastern Pakistan, the Hardwicke's Hedgehog is from the breeds of hedgehogs that have longer ears. They are usually very small, ranging in length from 6 to 8 inches and in weight from 200 to 500 grams. The dark brown underbelly is the same brown as the banded quills. The average lifespan for the Hardwicke's Hedgehog is 5 years.

Indian Hedgehog: Native to India and Pakistan, the Indian Hedgehog is a very small hedgehog that ranges in weight from 300 to 400 grams and in size from 5 to 7 inches. They have a lifespan of roughly 4 years. The hedgehog has a very pointy nose that is less snout-like than other hedgehog species. They should have pale brown colouring with a dark brown face mask and dark brown legs. In addition, the

Indian Hedgehogs have a greyish white stripe on their forehead.

Long-Eared Hedgehog: This small hedgehog is quite unique as it has very long, flexible ears. In addition, the hedgehog, weighing between 300 to 700 grams and reaching 7 to 10 inches in length, have fairly long legs for a hedgehog. They are native to Libya, Pakistan, Iraq, Israel and Iran. They are a light brown in colour and usually live about 5 years.

Somalian Hedgehog: Another of the smaller species of hedgehog, the Somalian Hedgehog is native to Northern Somalia. It usually measures between 7 to 10 inches in length and will weigh between 300 to 700 grams. It has chocolate and black banded quills and has two colours of fur on its underbelly. White is seen on most of the underbelly, while the rear part is brown. The average lifespan of a Somalian Hedgehog is about 5 years.

South African Hedgehog: Native to Zimbabwe, Zambia and South Africa, the South African Hedgehog is a small hedgehog with chocolate brown and black banded quills. There should be greyish brown fur on the belly and a pronounced band of white fur on the forehead. Their average lifespan is about 4 years and the average length is 7 to 10 inches. The South African Hedgehog usually weighs between 300 to 700 grams.

Western European Hedgehog: The Western European Hedgehog is native to Britain, Southern Scandinavia, Ireland and Western Europe. They are generally between 12 to 15 inches in length and they often weigh between 700 to 1000 grams. They have a lifespan of about 5 years. The Western European Hedgehop is characterized by the chocolate brown colouring on the banded quills and they should have brown fur on their belly.

Whilst it may seem that there are a lot of options for hedgehog owners from these species, generally, only the hybrid of the Algerian Hedgehog and the 4-Toed Hedgehog have been domesticated, although there are a few breeders who do offer other species of hedgehog.

History of the African Pygmy Hedgehog

As I mentioned in the last section on the types of hedgehogs, the African Pygmy Hedgehog is actually the domesticated hybrid of the Algerian Hedgehog and the 4-Toed Hedgehog.

Although hedgehogs have been kept for thousands of years and have been linked back to Ancient Rome, the actual practice of domesticating them became popular in the early 1980's. Before that time, owning a hedgehog was quite unheard of and when they were kept, it was primarily for meat and also for various uses of their quills.

In the 1980's, however, the African Pygmy Hedgehog was developed by crossing two African species of hedgehog, the Algerian Hedgehog and the 4-Toed Hedgehog.

Despite the term domestication, hedgehogs are not completely tamed. While efforts have been made over the years to breed out some of their fear reactions and some of their "wild" instincts, they still have many of these behaviours.

Over the years, breeders began to introduce different colours and patterns to the domesticated hedgehog and today, they are as diverse and varied as their personalities.

Appearance of a Hedgehog

As you know, in the beginning of this chapter, I went over the different types of hedgehog but when we talk about hedgehogs as pets, we are actually referring to the African Pygmy Hedgehog, which, as I already stated, is a hybrid of the Algerian Hedgehog and the 4-Toed Hedgehog.

The result of this pairing was a smaller hedgehog that weighs between 250 to 500 grams and 5 to 8 inches in length. Although they may seem to be a bit larger due to their quills, African Pygmy Hedgehogs are usually about the size of a small guinea pig.

They are characterized by their small racoon like faces. The African Pygmy hedgehog has a broad forehead and well-defined cheeks. This gives him a very cheerful appearance and it is highlighted by the small, black eyes and the pointy nose.

Hedgehogs have short, soft fur on their head, chest, legs and belly. The most identifiable trait of the hedgehog is the quills that cover their back. These quills are used primarily for defence and while they are technically described as modified hairs; they are actually a strong deterrent against predators.

Although it may not appear so, an adult hedgehog has roughly 7000 quills on their back. These quills are smooth and do not have any barb at the end. What they do have is a needle-like point that thickens as it reaches towards the body of the hedgehog and then tapers to a thin stem. Under the skin, there is a ball like follicle that holds the quill in place and allows for it to be raised with ease. They are made of air filled chambers so they are extremely light weight.

An African Pygmy Hedgehog that is at rest will have their quills lying down. These quills will cover a very small nub of a tail and this often leads many to believe that the hedgehog is tailless. If the hedgehog feels threatened, they will curl up their body. This causes two muscles on either side of their bodies to contract, which makes the quills move into an upright position. The end result is a tight ball of quills that crisscross together. Curled up, a hedgehog looks very similar to a sea urchin.

One thing that should be stressed is that a hedgehog does not fire quills at people. In addition, the quills are not barbed so they will not stick into the skin and stay there.

Colouring

Although colouring should be described with appearance, it is important to note that there are several differences in colour with African Pygmy Hedgehogs.

The very first thing that you should look at is the colouring of the quills. Most quills have a banded colouring, which is where there is more than one colour on the quill. With hedgehogs, they generally have a light colour, usually white, at the top and bottom of the quill. In the middle of the quill is a darker colour, usually brown in most species. This mottled colouring allows for camouflage from predators in the wild.

Outside of banding, colouring can vary greatly and I will go over the many different types of colours that you can get.

Albino: True to the word, albino hedgehogs are pure white. There is no pigmentation in the skin, nose or fur. The hair is white, and the quills are not banded but instead, are white as well. The skin and nose should be pink and the eyes of the albino African Pygmy Hedgehog are red.

Algerian Apricot: The Algerian Apricot has banded quills of cream and pale orange. The shoulders are pink but it is important to note that there is a hint of grey in the colouring. The light underbelly fur should be free of mottling. The eyes are a very deep ruby red and can often be mistaken for black. The nose should be a pink rimmed in pale liver. The Algerian Apricot should have no mask but there should be a slight presence of pale orangey-brown cheeks.

Algerian Apricot Snowflake: This colouring should be the same as the Algerian Apricot; however, 30 to 70% of the quills should be a solid white or cream colour. In addition, the hedgehog should have banded quills of cream and pale orange. The shoulders are pink but it is important to note that there is a hint of grey in the colouring. The light underbelly fur should be free of mottling. The eyes are a very deep ruby red and can often be mistaken for black. The nose should be a pink rimmed in pale liver. The Algerian Apricot should have no mask but there should be a slight presence of pale orangey-brown cheeks.

Algerian Apricot White: The Algerian Apricot White has banded quills of cream, and pale apricot. The remaining 95 to 97% of the quills should be a solid white or cream without any banding. The shoulders are pink but it is important to note that there is a hint of grey in the colouring. The light underbelly fur should be free of mottling. The eyes are a very deep ruby red and can often be mistaken for black. The nose should be a pink rimmed in pale liver. The Algerian Apricot should have no mask but there should be a slight presence of pale orangey-brown cheeks.

Algerian Black: This is a darker hedgehog with banded quills that are black, rust and cream. The fur is a mottled black with jet-black shoulders. The nose and eyes should be a dark black and the face should have a black mask that extends onto the quills around the head.

Algerian Black and White: The Algerian Black and White should have quills that are cream with black and rust bands. It is important to note that 95 to 97% of the quills should be a solid white with no banding. The shoulders are jet-black. The underbelly should be a dark black and should be heavily mottled. The eyes and nose should be black. The face should have a black mask that extends onto the quills around the head.

Algerian Black Snowflake: The black snowflake has the same colouring of the Algerian Black; however, 30 to 70% of the quills should be a solid white or cream colour. In addition, the hedgehog should have banded quills that are black, rust and cream. The fur on the underbelly is a mottled black with jet-black shoulders. The nose and eyes should be a dark black and the face should have a black mask that extends onto the quills around the head.

Algerian Brown: The Algerian Brown is a medium brown hedgehog with banded quills of cream and light brown. The shoulders are a dark grey and the underbelly fur is lightly mottled. The eyes are black and the nose is light chocolate brown with a small ring of darker chocolate. The mask is medium brown.

Algerian Brown Snowflake: This colouring should be the same as the Algerian Brown; however, 30 to 70% of the quills should be a solid white or cream colour. In addition, the hedgehog should have banded quills of cream and light brown. The shoulders are a dark grey and the underbelly fur is lightly mottled. The eyes are black and the nose is light chocolate brown with a small ring of darker chocolate. The mask is medium brown.

Algerian Brown White: The Algerian Brown White has banded quills of cream, and light brown on the forehead and a small part of the body. The remaining 95 to 97% of the quills should be a solid white or cream without any banding. The shoulders are a dark grey and the underbelly fur is lightly mottled. The eyes are black and the nose is light chocolate brown with a small ring of darker chocolate. The mask is medium brown.

Algerian Champagne: The Algerian Champagne has banded quills of cream and orange but they should have a light grey hue to them. The shoulders are a greyish pink and the underbelly fur is lightly coloured. The eyes are a very deep ruby red and can often be mistaken for black. The nose should be a mottled colouring of pink and grey. The mask is very pale and there should be a very light orange cheek patch on either cheek.

Algerian Champagne Snowflake: This colouring should be the same as the Algerian Champagne; however, 30 to 70% of the quills should be a solid white or cream colour. In addition, the hedgehog should have banded quills of cream and orange but they should have a light grey hue to them. The shoulders are a greyish pink and the underbelly fur is lightly coloured. The eyes are a very deep ruby red and can often be mistaken for black. The nose should be a mottled colouring of pink and grey. The mask is very pale and there should be a very light orange cheek patch on either cheek.

Algerian Champagne White: The Algerian Champagne White has banded quills of cream, and orange with a light grey hue to them on the forehead and a small part of the body. The remaining 95 to 97% of the quills should be a solid white or cream without any banding. The shoulders are a greyish pink and the underbelly fur is lightly coloured. The eyes are a very deep ruby red and can often be mistaken for black. The nose should be a mottled colouring of pink and grey. The mask is very pale and there should be a very light orange cheek patch on either cheek.

Algerian Charcoal White: The Algerian Charcoal White has banded quills of cream, black and rust on the forehead and a small part of the body. The remaining 95 to 97% of the quills should be a solid white or cream without any banding. The mottled belly is light in colour and the large, oversized mask, which goes into the cheeks, is a golden brown in colour. Eyes and nose should be black and the skin on the shoulders should be jet-black.

Algerian Chocolate: A dark brown hedgehog that have cream and chocolate brown banded quills. The heavily mottled belly is cream in colour and the skin on the shoulders is a dark grey. The eyes should be black but the nose should be dark chocolate in colour. The mask is brown but there should be lighter brown, to golden-brown eye patches around the eyes.

Algerian Chocolate Chip: This colouring should be the same as the Algerian Chocolate; however, 30 to 70% of the quills should be a solid white or cream colour. In addition, the hedgehog should have cream and chocolate brown banded quills. The heavily mottled belly is cream in colour and the skin on the shoulders is a dark grey. The eyes should be black but the nose should be dark chocolate in colour. The mask is brown but there should be lighter brown, to golden-brown eye patches around the eyes.

Algerian Chocolate White: The Algerian Pale Apricot has banded quills of cream, and dark chocolate on the forehead and a small part of the body. The remaining 95 to 97% of the quills should be a solid white or cream without any banding. The heavily mottled belly is cream in colour and the skin on the shoulders is a dark grey. The eyes should be black but the nose should be dark chocolate in colour. The mask is brown but there should be lighter brown, to golden-brown eye patches around the eyes.

Algerian Cinnamon: The Algerian Cinnamon has banded quills of cream and orange, that are similar to a cinnamon colour. The shoulders are grey and the underbelly fur is lightly mottled. The eyes are black and the nose is chocolate brown with a lighter liver colour throughout. The mask is very pale and there should be a very light brown cheek patch on either cheek.

Algerian Cinnamon Snowflake: This colouring should be the same as the Algerian Cinnamon; however, 30 to 70% of the quills should be a solid white or cream colour. In addition, the hedgehog should have banded quills of cream and orange, that are similar to a cinnamon colour. The shoulders are grey and the underbelly fur is lightly mottled. The eyes are black and the nose is chocolate brown with lighter liver colour throughout. The mask is very pale and there should be a very light brown cheek patch on either cheek.

Algerian Cinnamon White: The Algerian Cinnamon White has banded quills of cream, and a cinnamon orange on the forehead and a small part of the body. The remaining 95 to 97% of the quills should be a solid white or cream without any banding. The shoulders are grey and the underbelly fur is lightly mottled. The eyes are black and the nose is chocolate brown with lighter liver colour throughout. The mask is very pale and there should be a very light brown cheek patch on either cheek.

Algerian Cinnicot: The Algerian Cinnicot has banded quills of cream and orange, that is similar to a cinnamon colour. A few of the quills are also banded with an apricot colour and the majority should be banded. The shoulders are grey and the underbelly fur is a light cream colour and should be free of mottling. The eyes are pink and the nose is mottled with liver, grey and pink. The mask is very pale and there should be a very light brown cheek patch on either cheek.

Algerian Cinnicot Snowflake: This colouring should be the same as the Algerian Cinnamon; however, 30 to 70% of the quills should be a solid white or cream colour. In addition, the hedgehog should have banded quills of cream and orange, that are similar to a cinnamon colour. A few of the quills are also banded with an apricot colour and the majority should be banded. The shoulders are grey and the underbelly fur is a light cream colour and should be free of mottling. The eyes are pink and the nose is mottled with liver, grey and pink. The mask is very pale and there should be a very light brown cheek patch on either cheek.

Algerian Cinnicot White: The Algerian Cinnicot White has banded quills of cream, and a cinnamon orange or cream and apricot on the forehead and a small part of the body. The remaining 95 to 97% of the quills should be a solid white or cream without any banding. The shoulders are grey and the underbelly fur is a light cream colour and should be free of mottling. The eyes are pink and the nose is mottled with liver, grey and pink. The mask is very pale and there should be a very light brown cheek patch on either cheek.

Algerian Dark Cinnicot: The Algerian Dark Cinnicot has banded quills of cream and orange, that are similar to a very dark cinnamon colour. A few of the quills are also banded with a dark apricot colour and the majority should be banded. The shoulders are grey and the underbelly fur is a light cream colour and should be free of mottling. The eyes are black and the nose is mottled with liver and chocolate brown. The mask is very pale and there should be a very light brown cheek patch on either cheek.

Algerian Dark Cinnicot Snowflake: This colouring should be the same as the Algerian Dark Cinnicot; however, 30 to 70% of the quills should be a solid white or cream colour. In addition, the hedgehog should have banded quills of cream and orange, that are similar to a very dark cinnamon colour. A few of the quills are also banded with a dark apricot colour and the majority should be banded. The shoulders are grey and the underbelly fur is a light cream colour and should be free of mottling. The eyes are black and the nose is mottled with liver and chocolate brown. The mask is very pale and there should be a very light brown cheek patch on either cheek.

Algerian Dark Cinnicot White: The Algerian Dark Cinnicot White has banded quills of cream, and a cinnamon orange or cream and dark apricot on the forehead and a small part of the body. The remaining 95 to 97% of the quills should be a solid white or cream without any banding. The shoulders are grey and the underbelly fur is a light cream colour and should be free of mottling. The eyes are black and the nose is mottled with liver and chocolate brown. The mask is very pale and there should be a very light brown cheek patch on either cheek.

Algerian Dark Grey: This colouring is very similar to the Algerian Black with the cream quills banded with black and rust. In addition, there should be jet-black shoulders. Not all of the quills are banded and the belly should be a mottled black. The mask should be well defined and expands under the eyes. It should not extend onto the quills. The eyes and nose should be black.

Algerian Dark Grey Snowflake: The snowflake has the same colouring of the Algerian Dark Grey; however, 30 to 70% of the quills should be a solid white or cream colour. In addition, the hedgehog should have banded quills that are black, rust and cream. The fur on the underbelly is a mottled black with jet-black shoulders. Not all of the quills are banded and the belly should be a mottled black. The mask should be well defined and expands under the eyes. It should not extend onto the quills. The eyes and nose should be black.

Algerian Grey: This colouring is very similar to other Algerian colourings with the cream, black and rust banded quills. The main difference is that the mottled belly is lighter in colour and the large, oversized mask, which goes into the cheeks, is a golden brown in colour. Eyes and nose should be black and the skin on the shoulders should be jet-black.

Algerian Grey Snowflake: The snowflake has the same colouring of the Algerian Grey; however, 30 to 70% of the quills should be a solid white or cream colour. In addition, the hedgehog should have banded quills that are black, rust and cream. The mottled belly is light in colour and the large, oversized mask, which goes into the cheeks, is a golden brown in colour. Eyes and nose should be black and the skin on the shoulders should be jet-black.

Algerian Pale Apricot: The Algerian Pale Apricot has banded quills of cream and pale yellow or pale grey. The shoulders are pink but it is important to note that there is a hint of grey in the colouring. The light underbelly fur should be free of mottling. The eyes are ruby red. The nose should be a pink rimmed in pale liver. The Algerian Apricot should have no mask but there should be a slight presence of a pale orangey-brown muzzle.

Algerian Silver Charcoal White: The Algerian Silver Charcoal White has banded quills of cream, black and rust on the forehead and a small part of the body. The remaining 95 to 97% of the quills should be a solid white or cream without any banding. The shoulders are jet-black. The underbelly should be a dark black and should be heavily mottled. The mask should be well defined and expands under the eyes. It should not extend onto the quills. The eyes and nose should be black.

Apricot: The Apricot has white quills that are banded with a pale orange colour. The shoulders are pink. The eyes are red and the nose should be pink. The underbelly fur should be white with no mottling. The Apricot African Pygmy Hedgehog should have no mask.

Apricot Snowflake: The Apricot Snowflake should have 30% to 70% of their quills a solid white or cream colour. In addition, the hedgehog should have white quills that are banded with a pale orange colour. The shoulders are pink. The eyes are red and the nose should be pink. The underbelly fur should be white with no mottling. The Apricot Snowflake African Pygmy Hedgehog should have no mask.

Apricot White: Apricot White has white quills that are banded with a light orange. The banded quills are seen mostly on the forehead and a small part of the body. The remaining 95 to 97% of the quills should be a solid white or cream without any banding. The shoulders are pink. The eyes are red and the nose should be pink. The underbelly fur should be white with no mottling. The Apricot Snowflake African Pygmy Hedgehog should have no mask.

Black Eyed Cinnicot: The Black Eyed Cinnicot has white quills that are banded with a cinnamon brown and a pale apricot. It is important to note that 50% of the banded quills should be cinnamon brown while the remaining 50%

should be a pale apricot. The shoulders are pink. The eyes are black and the nose should be a mottled colour of pink and liver. The underbelly fur should be white and should be free of mottling. The Black Eyed Cinnicot African Pygmy Hedgehog should have no mask.

Black Eyed Cinnicot Snowflake: The Black Eyed Cinnicot Snowflake should have 30 to 70% of their quills a solid white or cream colour. In addition, the hedgehog should have white quills that are banded with a cinnamon brown and a pale apricot. It is important to note that 50% of the banded quills should be cinnamon brown while the remaining 50% should be a pale apricot. The shoulders are pink. The eyes are black and the nose should be a mottled colour of pink and liver. The underbelly fur should be white and should be free of mottling. The Black Eyed Cinnicot Snowflake African Pygmy Hedgehog should have no mask.

Black Eyed Cinnicot White: Black Eyed Cinnicot White has white quills that are banded with either cinnamon or dark apricot. It is important to note that 50% should be cinnamon with the remaining 50% of the banded quills being light apricot. The banded quills are seen mostly on the forehead and a small part of the body. The remaining 95 to 97% of the quills should be a solid white or cream without any banding. The shoulders are pink. The eyes are black and the nose should be a mottled colour of pink and liver. The underbelly fur should be white and should be free of mottling. The Black Eyed Cinnicot White African Pygmy Hedgehog should have no mask.

Brown: The Brown has white quills that are banded with light brown. The shoulders are pink but they should have a small amount of grey to the colouring. The eyes should be black and the nose should be chocolate brown. The underbelly fur should be white and free of mottling. The mask should be a light brown.

Brown Snowflake: The Brown Snowflake should have 30 to 70% of its quills a solid white or cream colour. In addition, the hedgehog should have white quills that are banded with light brown. The shoulders are pink but they should have a small amount of grey to the colouring. The eyes should be black and the nose should be chocolate brown. The underbelly fur should be white and free of mottling. There should be no mask.

Brown White: Brown White has white quills that are banded with a chocolate brown. The banded quills are seen mostly on the forehead and a small part of the body. The remaining 95 to 97% of the quills should be a solid white or cream without any banding. The shoulders are pink but they should have a small amount of grey to the colouring. The eyes should be black and the nose should be chocolate brown. The underbelly fur should be white and free of mottling. The mask should be light brown.

Champagne: The Champagne has white quills that are banded with cinnamon and pale orange taupe. It is important to note that 75% of the banded quills should be taupe while the remaining 25% should be cinnamon. The shoulders are pink. The eyes are red and the nose should be pink in colour with a rim of liver on the outer edges. The underbelly fur should be white and should be free of mottling. The Champagne African Pygmy Hedgehog should have no mask.

Champagne Snowflake: The Champagne Snowflake should have 30 to 70% of its quills a solid white or cream colour. In addition, the hedgehog should have white quills that are banded with cinnamon and pale orange taupe. It is important to note that 75% of the banded quills should be taupe while the remaining 25% should be cinnamon. The shoulders are pink. The eyes are red and the nose should be pink in colour with a rim of liver on the outer edges. The underbelly fur should be white and should be free of mottling. The Champagne Snowflake African Pygmy Hedgehog should have no mask.

Champagne White: Champagne White has white quills that are banded with either cinnamon or pale orange-taupe. It is important to note that 25% should be cinnamon with the remaining 75% of the banded quills being pale orange-taupe. The banded quills are seen mostly on the forehead and a small part of the body. The remaining 95 to 97% of the quills should be a solid white or cream without any banding. The eyes are red and the nose should be pink in colour with a rim of liver on the outer edges. The underbelly fur should be white and should be free of mottling. The Champagne White African Pygmy Hedgehog should have no mask.

Charcoal: The Charcoal should have 30 to 70% of his quills a solid white or cream colour. In addition, the hedgehog should have white quills that are banded with black and has a small hint of rust on the outer edges of the black. The shoulders are grey. The eyes and nose should be black. The underbelly fur should be white with some mottling. The mask is very small and should be black.

Charcoal White: Charcoal White has white quills that are banded with black and a very small line of rust on the outer edges of the black. They are seen mostly on the forehead and a small part of the body. The remaining 95 to 97% of the quills should be a solid white or cream without any banding. The shoulders are grey. The eyes and nose should be black. The underbelly fur should be white with some mottling. The mask is very small and should be black.

Chocolate: The Chocolate has white quills that are banded with a rich, dark chocolate brown. The shoulders are light grey. The eyes and nose should be black. The underbelly fur should be white with very pale mottling. The mask should be light brown.

Chocolate Chip: The Chocolate Chip should have 30 to 70% of his quills a solid white or cream colour. In addition, the hedgehog should have white quills that are banded with a rich, dark chocolate brown. The shoulders are a light grey. The eyes and nose should be black. The underbelly fur should be white and should be free of mottling. There should be no mask.

Chocolate White: Chocolate White has white quills that are banded with a chocolate brown. The banded quills are seen mostly on the forehead and a small part of the body. The remaining 95 to 97% of the quills should be a solid white or cream without any banding. The shoulders are light grey. The eyes and nose should be black. The underbelly fur should be white and should be free of mottling. There should be no mask.

Cinnamon: The Cinnamon has white quills that are banded with a cinnamon brown colour. The shoulders are pink. The eyes are black and the nose should be liver in colour. The underbelly fur should be white and should be free of mottling. The Cinnamon African Pygmy Hedgehog should have no mask.

Cinnamon Snowflake: The Cinnamon Snowflake should have 30 to 70% of their quills a solid white or cream colour. In addition, the hedgehog should have white quills that are banded with a cinnamon brown colour. The shoulders are pink. The eyes are black and the nose should be liver in colour. The underbelly fur should be white and should be free of mottling. The Cinnamon Snowflake African Pygmy Hedgehog should have no mask.

Dark Cinnicot: The Dark Cinnicot has white quills that are banded with a cinnamon brown and a dark apricot. It is important to note that 75% of the banded quills should be cinnamon brown while the remaining 25% should be apricot. The shoulders are pink. The eyes are black and the nose should be liver in colour with a rim of pink on the outer edges. The underbelly fur should be white and should be free of mottling. The Dark Cinnicot African Pygmy Hedgehog should have no mask.

Dark Cinnicot Snowflake: The Dark Cinnicot Snowflake should have 30 to 70% of its quills a solid white or cream colour. In addition, the hedgehog should have white quills that are banded with a cinnamon brown and a dark apricot. It is important to note that 75% of the banded quills should be cinnamon brown while the remaining 25% should be

apricot. The shoulders are pink. The eyes are black and the
nose should be liver in colour with a rim of pink on the
outer edges. The underbelly fur should be white and
should be free of mottling. The Dark Cinnicot Snowflake
African Pygmy Hedgehog should have no mask.

Dark Cinnicot White: Dark Cinnicot White has white
quills that are banded with either cinnamon or dark apricot.
It is important to note that 75% should be cinnamon with
the remaining 25% of the banded quills being dark apricot.
The banded quills are seen mostly on the forehead and a
small part of the body. The remaining 95 to 97% of the
quills should be a solid white or cream without any
banding. The shoulders are pink. The eyes are black and
the nose should be liver in colour with a rim of pink on the
outer edges. The underbelly fur should be white and
should be free of mottling. The Dark Cinnicot White
African Pygmy Hedgehog should have no mask.

Dark Grey: The Dark Grey has white quills that are banded
with black and has a small hint of rust on the outer edges of
the black. The shoulders are a dark grey. The eyes and nose
should be black. The underbelly fur should be white with
extensive black mottling. The mask is very small and
should be black.

Grey: The Grey has white quills that are banded with black
and has a small hint of rust on the outer edges of the black.
The shoulders are grey. The eyes and nose should be black.
The underbelly fur should be white with some mottling.
The mask is very small and should be black.

Pale Apricot: The Pale Apricot has white quills that are
banded with a light yellow to very pale orangey yellow
colour. The shoulders are pink. The eyes are red and the
nose should be pink. The underbelly fur should be white

with no mottling. The Pale Apricot African Pygmy Hedgehog should have no mask.

Pale Apricot Snowflake: The Pale Apricot Snowflake should have 30% to 70% of its quills a solid white or a cream colour. In addition, the hedgehog should have white quills that are banded with a light yellow to very pale orangey yellow colour. The shoulders are pink. The eyes are red and the nose should be pink. The underbelly fur should be white with no mottling. The Pale Apricot Snowflake African Pygmy Hedgehog should have no mask.

Pinto: Although it is classified as a specific colour, it is actually a pattern that consists of white colouring on the majority of the hedgehog and a dark, distinct patch of quills on the back. The best confirmation of the pinto pattern is when there is a symmetrical colouring with an equal amount of white on either side of a distinct patch.

Platinum: The Platinum has white quills that are banded with light grey on the forehead and a small part of the body. The remaining 95 to 97% of the quills should be a solid white or cream without any banding. The shoulders are jet black and so are the nose and the eyes. The underbelly fur should be white with extensive black mottling. The mask is very small and should be black.

Ruby Eyed Cinnicot: The Ruby Eyed Cinnicot has white quills that are banded with a cinnamon brown and a pale apricot. It is important to note that 50% of the banded quills should be cinnamon brown while the remaining 50% should be a pale apricot. The shoulders are pink. The eyes are dark ruby red and can sometimes be mistaken as black. The nose should be a mottled colour of pink and liver. The underbelly fur should be white and should be free of mottling. The Ruby Eyed Cinnicot African Pygmy Hedgehog should have no mask.

Ruby Eyed Cinnicot Snowflake: The Ruby Eyed Cinnicot Snowflake should have 30 to 70% of its quills a solid white or cream colour. In addition, the hedgehog should have white quills that are banded with a cinnamon brown and a pale apricot. It is important to note that 50% of the banded quills should be cinnamon brown while the remaining 50% should be a pale apricot. The shoulders are pink. The eyes are dark ruby red and can sometimes be mistaken as black. The nose should be a mottled colour of pink and liver. The underbelly fur should be white and should be free of mottling. The Ruby Eyed Cinnicot Snowflake African Pygmy Hedgehog should have no mask.

Ruby Eyed Cinnicot White: Ruby Eyed Cinnicot White has white quills that are banded with either cinnamon or dark apricot. It is important to note that 50% should be cinnamon with the remaining 50% of the banded quills being light apricot. The banded quills are seen mostly on the forehead and a small part of the body. The remaining 95 to 97% of the quills should be a solid white or cream without any banding. The shoulders are pink. The eyes are dark ruby red and can sometimes be mistaken as black. The nose should be a mottled colour of pink and liver. The underbelly fur should be white and should be free of mottling. The Ruby Eyed Cinnicot African Pygmy Hedgehog should have no mask.

Salt and Pepper: The Salt and Pepper has white quills that are banded by black. The shoulders are jet-black and so are the nose and eyes. The underbelly fur should be white with extensive black mottling. The mask is very small on the salt and pepper and should be black.

Silver: The Silver should have 30 to 70% of his quills a solid white or cream colour. In addition, the hedgehog should have white quills that are banded by black. The shoulders are jet black and so are the nose and the eyes. The underbelly fur should be white with extensive black mottling. The mask is very small on the salt and pepper and should be black.

Silver Charcoal: The Silver Charcoal should have 30 to 70% of its quills a solid white or cream colour. In addition, the hedgehog should have white quills that are banded with black and have a small hint of rust on the outer edges of the black. The shoulders are dark grey. The eyes and nose should be black. The underbelly fur should be white with extensive black mottling. The mask is very small and should be black.

Silver Charcoal White: Silver Charcoal White has white quills that are banded with black and a very small line of rust. They are seen mostly on the forehead and a small part of the body. The remaining 95 to 97% of the quills should be a solid white or cream without any banding. The shoulders are a dark grey. The eyes and nose should be black. The underbelly fur should be white with extensive black mottling. The mask is very small and should be black.

White: White has white quills that are banded with a cinnamon brown. The banded quills are seen mostly on the forehead and a small part of the body. The remaining 95 to 97% of the quills should be a solid white or cream without any banding. The shoulders are pink. The eyes are black and the nose should be liver in colour. The underbelly fur should be white and should be free of mottling. The Cinnamon African Pygmy Hedgehog should have no mask.

As you can see, there are a large assortment of colours and while they may seem similar, the colour difference between the colour variations, such as the 95% white in the Silver Charcoal White, can make the hedgehog look completely different from a Silver Charcoal, for example.

Character and Personality of a Hedgehog

Now that you know everything you need to know about the appearance of a hedgehog and the many different colours that you can find hedgehogs in, it is time to look at their different personality traits and characters.

Before I launch into their qualities, it is important to note that every hedgehog is slightly different.

Traits that are common in hedgehogs are:

- *Cheerful:* Most hedgehogs are described as being a very cheerful pet. They are very pleasant and, when properly socialized, can be a joy to take everywhere with you.

- *Alert:* Hedgehogs are usually very alert when they are awake and this is also what you would look for in a healthy hedgehog.

- *Peaceful:* Although we don't often think of the word peaceful when we think of pets, the hedgehog fits this word perfectly. They are often very quiet and have a very gentle disposition. They generally bond very closely to their owner and will be the perfect companion for their entire life.

- *Humorous:* Hedgehogs are known for having a bit of a sense of humour and this can make them a delightful pet to both spend time with and watch.

- *Playful:* Some hedgehogs are more playful than others but all of them enjoy playing and can be quite playful with their owners.

- *Solitary:* Hedgehogs are naturally solitary creatures and in the wild, they are not usually found with other hedgehogs. While you can own more than one hedgehog, it is better to have separate cages for them. Although they are solitary, hedgehogs often bond very well with their owners and will enjoy spending much of their time with them.

- *Nocturnal:* Later in this book, I look at ways to flip their schedules so they are less nocturnal, however, anyone who enjoys hedgehogs should be prepared for this trait.

Remember, there is no set temperament to expect. Some hedgehogs are playful, some like to cuddle and some are aloof. The key, when choosing a hedgehog is to find one that suits your personality so you are sure to have the perfect pet.

General Facts about Hedgehogs

Now that we have gone over everything you need to know to understand hedgehogs, it is time to look at a few general facts about hedgehogs. Later in this book, we will expand on everything concerning hedgehogs, but for now, let's look at some of the more commonly asked questions.

Do hedgehogs make good pets?

Yes, hedgehogs can make wonderful pets if they are properly socialized. They are very social creatures when properly handled and will often travel with their owners when they get the opportunity. In addition, they usually have a cheerful disposition and they are happy to cuddle with people or perform a few small tasks for a treat or two.

In addition, while they do need daily care, hedgehogs are not a high maintenance pet and are an excellent choice for those who want a sociable pet but do not want the high chores list that some other pets offer.

Are they good with children?

Hedgehogs do very well with children; however, they are better suited to older children. It is important that children know how to properly handle the hedgehog to prevent accidents from happening. In addition, children need to be calm around hedgehogs to prevent triggering a fear response.

Are they clean?

Yes, hedgehogs are surprisingly clean. They can be litter trained and they generally keep their cage clean. The main thing that you need to be aware of is that they do have the small mammal scent. If you keep the cage clean and tidy and use baking soda in the litter box, you can usually keep them fresh smelling.

Can they live in cold climates?

Yes, hedgehogs can live in cold and hot climates; however, it is very important to keep the temperature even. Too much heat and they can suffer from heat stroke, too much cold and they could become ill. In addition, cold will trigger hibernation and this can shorten your hedgehog's lifespan.

Are they noisy?

While they may not be as noisy as some pets, hedgehogs will chirp and make other noises throughout their day. The main problem with the noise is that hedgehogs are nocturnal so most of the noise they make is at night. If you find you are a light sleeper, do not place the hedgehog in your bedroom.

What is the lifespan of a hedgehog?

This varies from hedgehog to hedgehog, but on average, hedgehogs will usually live between 4 to 6 years. It is important to note that some have a shorter lifespan of only 3 years and others have lived to over 9 years. Be prepared to have this pet for a significant amount of time.

Are there different types of hedgehogs?

While there are 14 different species of hedgehogs, there is actually only one type of hedgehog that has been domesticated and that is the African Pygmy Hedgehog.

How big do hedgehogs get?

As I have already mentioned earlier in this chapter, hedgehogs reach between 250 to 500 grams in weight and 5 to 8 inches in length. It is important to note that some breeders are producing larger hedgehogs that can reach up to 12 inches in length and 2 pounds in weight but the standard hedgehog size is the smaller variety.

How long do they take to mature?

If you are looking at breeding age, a hedgehog is considered to be mature by about 8 weeks of age, however, that is not when they are fully mature. In addition, hedgehogs should never be bred at 8 weeks of age. With maturity, it usually takes 10 to 11 months before a hedgehog has reached full maturity.

Chapter Three: Are you ready to Raise Hedgehogs?

Despite the fact that hedgehogs are a wonderful pet, they are not for everyone. There are some challenges that they can present, which I will go over later in this book, and they do require daily care and handling. A hedgehog that is simply left in their cage will quickly become despondent.

Before you purchase a hedgehog, make sure that you ask yourself a few questions to determine if you are ready for one.

Are they legal in your area?

The very first thing that you should ask is whether the hedgehog is legal in your area or not. Some states and countries have banned hedgehogs due to the fear of release into the wild. Make sure that you understand the laws concerning hedgehogs in your area and that you also check to see if you need any special permits to own them.

Do you rent or own?

This may not seem like a huge problem when you consider that hedgehogs are a small pet and reside mainly in a cage, but some rentals have rules against any type of pet. If you rent, make sure that hedgehogs are allowed in your tenant agreement before you purchase.

What type of dwelling do you live in?

Hedgehogs can live in any type of building but remember that their cages do require a bit of room so they may not be ideal for a small dwelling. Still, if you have the space for their cage, a hedgehog can live anywhere.

Do you have the time?

As I have mentioned already, hedgehogs are not pets that require a lot of maintenance but they do require a fair amount of time. These are pets that need to be handled several times per day. In addition, they need fresh food and water daily and they need to be exercised out of their cage. Generally, you should expect to spend at least 2 hours every day caring for the needs of your hedgehog pet.

Are you looking for an affectionate pet?

Although hedgehogs can be affectionate with their owners, it is not a pet that I would recommend if you are looking for a very affectionate pet. Remember that they still have many of the fear drives that their wild counterparts have. They will cuddle once socialization is done; however, this is something that takes time and a lot of effort.

Do you have access to a small mammal vet?

Hedgehogs do require regular check-ups with a veterinarian and I strongly recommend having access to a small animal vet. Emergencies can arise so make sure his medical needs will be taken care of.

Do you have the funds?

While hedgehogs may not be expensive compared to other pets, there is still a high cost to properly set up a cage for your hedgehog. In addition, there are food and medical costs that you should be prepared for.

Do you have the ability to find food?

Later in this book, I will go over the food that your hedgehog will need and while most of it can be purchased very easily, you need to be prepared to feed live insects to your hedgehog. If you are a bit squeamish and don't think you can handle the live food, then you should probably choose a different pet.

Can you provide the proper safety for your pet?

Lastly, make sure that you can provide the proper safety for your hedgehog. This means a proper cage, proper supervision when your hedgehog is out and proper medical care. In addition, if you have other pets, make sure that you keep your hedgehog safe from them.

Hedgehogs can make wonderful pets but you should be prepared for their unique needs, which we look at throughout this book.

Pros and Cons of Owning Hedgehogs

Like every other type of animal, there are a number of pros and cons that you should consider before you purchase your own hedgehog and I will go over both of them to help you make the best decision.

Pros of Owning an African Pygmy Hedgehog

- *Sweet Temperament:* One of the biggest pros of owning a hedgehog is that they have a very sweet and personable temperament. Some can be a bit cantankerous but most are very gentle and happy.

- *Unique:* If you are looking for a unique pet, then there are few pets that are quite as unique as a

  hedgehog. These are exotic pets and while they are gaining popularity, they are still fairly rare.

- *Cute:* Some people find hedgehogs to be a little frightening with their quills but their sweet, racoon like faces make them quite cute.

- *Funny:* Hedgehogs are really funny and entertaining to watch.

- *Inexpensive:* On average, the daily care for hedgehogs is really inexpensive. They don't need a lot of food and the food they do use is often very cheap.

- *Easy to Care for:* Hedgehogs are usually very easy to care for. They do require daily handling and daily feeding, but they do not require a lot of other care.

- *Low Smell:* While their litter box can smell, the hedgehog itself does not have a strong odour. If you keep the cage clean, the amount of odour should be very low.

- *Can be Litter Trained:* Hedgehogs can be litter trained very easily.

- *Take up Little Space:* Finally, hedgehogs take up very little space, especially if you design their cage properly.

One thing that most hedgehog owners agree on is that owning a hedgehog is a very rewarding experience.

Cons of Owning an African Pygmy Hedgehog

- *Nocturnal:* One of the biggest cons to owning a hedgehog is that they are nocturnal animals. This means that they will be moving around at night and that they will be less than happy to be bothered during the day.

- *Illegal in Some Areas:* As I have already mentioned, hedgehogs are illegal in some areas so it is important to make sure you can't get into any trouble if you own one.

- *Quills:* Although the quills are one of the traits that make them such a unique pet, hedgehogs will use them if they feel threatened. Be prepared to feel the quill a few times, especially when your hedgehog is first being socialized.

- *Need Daily Handling:* Hedgehogs need to be handled on a daily basis to make sure that they are properly socialized. This can be a bit time consuming and if you are simply looking for a pet to leave in a cage, the hedgehog is not for you.

- *Need Even Temperatures:* Hedgehogs are susceptible to extreme shifts in temperature in either direction and it can be difficult to give them the ideal temperature that they need.

- *Are Not Social:* While hedgehogs can learn to be very social and affectionate with their owners, they are not usually that way with other people. In addition, they need to be in separate cages as they prefer to be on their own.

- *Are Not Pet Friendly:* You can own hedgehogs with other pets but you will need to keep them separate. These are animals that trigger prey drives in both cats and dogs and they will react defensively. Allowing other pets to interact with your hedgehog can lead to significant vet bills for all involved.

- *Difficulty Finding Care:* Lastly, it can be difficult to find a veterinarian for your hedgehog. This will often mean higher medical costs as you will need to travel further for specialists.

As with all animals, it is important to understand both the challenges and advantages of owning and raising African Pygmy Hedgehogs. Owning them can be wonderful but it is a commitment and shouldn't be entered into lightly.

Chapter Four: Choosing the Right Hedgehog

As you know, the very first step to bringing your hedgehog home is in selecting the proper hedgehog. Earlier in this book, I mentioned that this book primarily deals with African Pygmy Hedgehogs but many of the tips and advice can be applied to any type of hedgehog.

The same is true for choosing your hedgehog and I will go over everything you need to know about picking a breeder and ultimately picking your own hedgehog.

Finding a Breeder

When it comes to finding a breeder, it can actually be a very easy task. Although hedgehogs are an exotic pet that are not enjoyed by as many owners as dogs or cats, there are still enough breeders around to locate them very easily.

In fact, I always recommend that you visit hedgehog groups online to find the breeder of your hedgehog. It is important to note that not all areas will have a breeder and you may have to arrange transportation for your hedgehog, although be aware that transporting can be detrimental to the hedgehog's health.

Before you look for a breeder, it is important to understand the different places where you can purchase a hedgehog. These are:

- *Pet Stores:* Some pet stores do carry hedgehogs and it can make it very easy to purchase one in your area. One of the biggest negatives of purchasing a hedgehog from a pet store is that often, the stock is not as healthy and the hedgehogs have not been properly socialized.

- *Flea Markets:* Surprisingly, flea markets are a great place to find hedgehogs, again, there are many negatives to purchasing a hedgehog at a flea market and often it comes down to the hedgehogs being unhealthy.

- *Animal Sales:* Animal sales are another great place to locate them and many times you can find some excellent breeders at animal sales. My only recommendation would be to make contact with a breeder at an animal sale and then set up going to them to purchase the hedgehog. The main reason for this is so you can ensure that your hedgehog is coming from a clean and responsible breeder.

- *Breeders:* The one that I recommend the most is to find a breeder near your location and purchase your African Pygmy Hedgehog from a reputable one. This is one of the best ways to ensure that the hedgehog is healthy and well socialized. You can find hedgehog breeders in classified ads, on the internet or through several hedgehog organizations including:
  - Hedgehog Central
  - Hedgehog Breeder's Alliance
  - Worldwide Hedgehog Breeder's List
  - Hedgehog World

Once you have narrowed down where you can purchase your hedgehog, it is important to look at some traits that you will want in your breeder. One thing that I should emphasise is that you should never choose the cheapest option unless it is clearly the better option. Purchasing an inexpensive pet often leads to many problems for the purchaser so make sure that your hedgehog's breeder is reputable and is trying to produce a quality pet.

What to Look for when Buying

If you are purchasing a hedgehog from other places than a hedgehog breeder, you may not be able to look at everything on this list. Instead, you should try to look at the overall health of the hedgehogs but you can also check off a few of the traits on this list, even at a pet store.

- *Clean Environment:* When you go to purchase your hedgehog, make sure that the environment of the breeder is clean. Also make sure that the hedgehogs are kept in clean, spacious cages. If it looks dirty in any way, or the hedgehogs look like they are in a cramped environment, look elsewhere for your hedgehog.

- *Separated:* In addition to clean and spacious cages, make sure that the animals are housed separately or in gender groups. This means that males are only housed with males and so on. If you find that the male and female hedgehogs have been kept together after they are 8 weeks of age, avoid purchasing a female from that breeder or you may be in for a small surprise.

- *Proper Age:* Make sure that the hedgehogs are the proper age when they are bred. Although they can be bred as young as 8 weeks old, you should never purchase a hedgehog from a mother or father that is younger than 5 months of age. In addition, never purchase from a mother that is over 3 and a half years old.

- *Knowledgeable Breeder:* Another thing you should look for is if the breeder or the sales person is knowledgeable about hedgehogs. Can they answer your questions? Do they offer advice? Make sure that the breeder knows and understands hedgehogs before you purchase from them.

- *Proper Diet:* When you are checking on the housing of the breeding hedgehogs, make sure that the animals are eating a good quality diet that is also versatile.

- *Proper Socialization:* I mention this repeatedly throughout the book but make sure that the hedgehog babies are being properly handled and socialized. If the babies are not handled every 30 minutes to an hour during their active time, then you should choose a different breeder.

- *Healthy Hedgehogs:* Make sure that the hedgehogs look healthy when you look at them. It is important for the parents to look as healthy as the young, since the health of the parents will affect the health of their babies.

- *Additional Support:* One of the biggest draws to purchasing from a hedgehog breeder is that many will offer you support after your hedgehog goes home. This means that you can ask any questions that you have. I strongly recommend finding a breeder who offers this to you.

The main thing that you should remember when you are choosing a breeder is to find one that you feel comfortable with. If you find the area seems dirty or the hedgehogs are unhealthy, find a different breeder.

In addition, find one that will take the time to demonstrate how to handle and hold your hedgehog. Make sure that he also takes the time to show you how to sex the hedgehog, and determine what the gender is, since this is very important as well.

If you follow these guidelines, you are sure to have a healthy hedgehog.

Choosing your Hedgehog

Now that you know what to look for in a hedgehog breeder, it is now time to understand what you should look for in your African Pygmy Hedgehog. Remember that starting with a reputable and responsible breeder is the key to successfully finding the hedgehog that is perfect for you.

Before you choose your own hedgehog, there are a few things that you should consider and I will go over them in this section.

Male or Female?

The very first thing that you should ask yourself is whether you should have a male or female. In general, there are not a lot of differences between males and females. Both can be equally entertaining and they can both be a charming companion.

With personality, sex does not determine whether or not the animal will bond with an owner. In fact, gender really has no difference in the personality of the hedgehog and you should never base your decision on how a male will be different to a female in personality.

The main reason why you should consider whether you are ready for a male or a female is because of health reasons. Males, although many can be healthy, usually have a higher risk of developing health problems than females do.

They have a greater risk of urinary tract infections and also have a higher risk of developing kidney stones.

In addition, it is very important for owners to constantly check the external sheath of their genitalia to check for any signs of infection.

Another problem that males can present is the habit of playing with themselves. Not all males do this but a large number will and you will find that you need to remove the white discharge from their belly on a regular basis.

With females, hedgehogs are at a higher risk for reproductive cancers such as uterine contractions. It is important to note that spaying is possible but it is a very expensive procedure and it can put the hedgehog at an unnecessary risk during the surgery.

In the end, there are positives and negatives to owning both males and females but it is important to decide for yourself which is the better choice for you.

Sexing a Hedgehog

When you are selecting a hedgehog, most breeders will determine the gender of your hedgehog. This is known as sexing but I recommend that everyone learns how to do this.

To sex your hedgehog, place him in your hand and turn him over so his belly is showing. Hold his tail out of the way if you need to but try to avoid handling him too much or he may roll up into himself. Directly under the tail, you should see a space between the genitals and the rectum. If it looks like there is a belly button in that space, which is created by a large gap there, then it is a male hedgehog. If there is no gap and the genitals are close to the rectum, then it is a female.

Age of the Hedgehog?

If you are new to the world of hedgehogs, I strongly recommend that you start with a young hedgehog. The reason for this is because hedgehogs do not bond as easily when they are older and you will not experience the full enjoyment of a hedgehog.

With age, you should make sure that the hedgehog is no younger than 8 weeks of age. Bringing a hedgehog home sooner than 8 weeks can be detrimental to the health of the hedgehog and it can damage the bond that you are trying to build with it. In general, I recommend choosing a hedgehog that is between the ages of 8 weeks to 3 months for first time owners.

How many to Choose?

Although it can be tempting, never purchase more than one hedgehog unless you have the cages set up for them. Remember, these are solitary creatures and they do not do well in a cage with multiple hedgehogs. In addition, you should never put a male and female together unless your intention is to breed them.

If you are new to hedgehogs, purchase one the first time and then add to your home once you and your new hedgehog have bonded.

What Type of Temperament?

Although your choice in temperament will really depend on what you are personally looking for, when you are choosing a hedgehog, look for one that is friendly but do not feel as though they have to be really friendly.

African Pygmy Hedgehog

In fact, when you are selecting your hedgehog, pick it up. If it begins hissing, don't be alarmed, this is completely normal and does not mean that you should choose a different hedgehog. In addition, a hedgehog will usually roll up when it is handled by a stranger. However, if you find that the hedgehog does not start to relax after a few minutes of being held, you may want to choose a different hedgehog.

Another thing you will want to avoid is a hedgehog that begins clicking at you. This is a sign that the hedgehog is trying to threaten you and it will mean that bonding with the hedgehog will be harder.

When you are selecting a hedgehog according to temperament, make sure you talk with the breeder. He will be able to tell you which hedgehog is playful and which one is calm and loves to cuddle. After talking with him, it will be much easier to choose a hedgehog that matches both your lifestyle and you.

Health of the Hedgehog?

The last thing that you should do when choosing your African Pygmy Hedgehog is to look at the actual health of the hedgehog. Remember to check on the adults at the breeder's when you arrive but also check all the littermates of the hedgehog you will be purchasing.

It may seem odd to look at animals you have no intention on purchasing, but if you find there are sick animals in the litter or at the breeders, then it is a good indicator to look elsewhere for a hedgehog.

When you are doing a health check of your hedgehog, it is important to look at the following:

- *Eyes:* Eyes should be bright and alert. Make sure that you go to the breeders in the evening so you can see the hedgehog when he is active. African Pygmy Hedgehogs have round; beady eyes that should be wide open when he is alert. If they are not, avoid purchasing that hedgehog.

- *Ears:* Along with the eyes, it is important to look at the hedgehog's ear. Make sure that it is short, round and clean and there are no tatters to it. If you see any chew marks on the ear, don't worry as long as it has healed. Chew marks are very common since hedgehog babies will bite each other.

- *Nose:* Make sure that the nose is free of any discharge.

- *No Quills Missing:* Check over the back of the hedgehog and make sure no quills are missing. If you are purchasing a hedgehog between 4 months to 6 months of age, you may find some of the quills missing due to quilling, which is when they lose their quills, discuss it with the hedgehog breeder. Some hedgehogs will begin quilling by the age of 8 weeks old. If it is outside of those ages and you see large chunks of quills missing, then it can be an indicator of a parasite such as fleas or mites and you should look for a different breeder.

- *Steady Walking:* Take the time to have the hedgehog walk around on a flat surface when you get there. Watch it for a few minutes and make sure there is no wobbling and that it is steady on its feet. If the hedgehog isn't, choose a different hedgehog.

- *Healthy Weight:* A hedgehog should be plump but it should never be obese in size. If you feel that the hedgehog is too skinny or too fat, find a different hedgehog to purchase.

- *Soft Belly Fur:* Touch the belly fur and make sure that it is soft and moves when you touch it. If it is hard, or is matted, then it could be sings of a parasite or illness.

- *Clear Breathing:* Finally, check to make sure the hedgehog is breathing clearly. If you hear a slight rattle, it could be an indication of illness. Remember that hedgehogs can be quite vocal so make sure that you are not mistaking his usual chatter for a rattle.

Remember that you should always make sure you feel comfortable with the purchase. If you ever feel that something is wrong, don't purchase that specific hedgehog.

It is better for you and the hedgehog if you have no second doubts about the overall quality or health of the hedgehog. In addition, going with your gut instinct will really help you steer clear of purchasing a hedgehog with potential health problems.

Chapter Five: Preparing for your Hedgehog

One of the first steps that any new hedgehog owner should take is the step of preparing for your hedgehog. While hedgehogs are considered to be a small pet, they are not something that you should simply make a spur of the moment purchase on. These are pets that do best when their owners properly prepare for them.

In this next chapter, I will go over everything you need to know about your hedgehog's cage, where to place it and how to furnish it. Once you are prepared for your hedgehog, bringing him home will be an easy transition for both you and your pet.

Your Hedgehog's Cage

The cage that your hedgehog will be living in is a very important factor in creating the perfect living condition for your pet. There are many factors that need to be taken into consideration and these are:

- *Size:* While they are a fairly small animal, hedgehogs do require a cage with enough room to move around. Generally, you want a cage that is about 18 by 24 inches in size, usually about the same size as a dwarf bunny's cage.

- *Materials:* It is recommended that you choose a cage that can be cleaned easily. Metal trays work much better than many other types of material. Regardless of the material, make sure that your cage is made with high quality and pet safe materials.

- *Durability:* This falls under materials, make sure that you choose a cage that is durable. Remember that hedgehogs have a lifespan of up to 10 years and you want to have a cage that can last for most of those years.

- *Solid:* Although there are some recommendations to have a mesh floor on your hedgehog cage, you should avoid this completely. It is very easy for your hedgehog's feet to fall through the mesh and could lead to serious injuries.

One thing that should be stressed is that hedgehog owners are at a disadvantage when selecting cages. While the popularity of African Pygmy Hedgehogs is growing, they are still unusual enough for there to be no standard cage designed for them. This means that hedgehog owners are left with the problem of either choosing a cage designed for a different animal or choosing to make their own cage.

When you are choosing your cage, again, make sure that it has the appropriate size. Hedgehogs need about 4 feet of square footage to thrive but it does not have to be a one level cage. In fact, they can do very well in a multi-level cage and this is something that I would recommend whether you have the

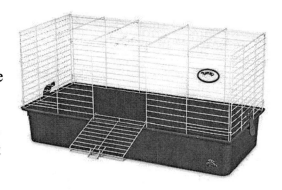

space for a large cage or not.

When you do a multilevel cage, make sure that all of the levels are enclosed. Also, make sure the ramps are enclosed as well. Hedgehogs can be prone to falling so it is important to prevent this with enclosed levels and ramps.

Wire cages can be excellent for hedgehogs, but again, make sure that the bottom is solid, either through the use of a tray or simply designed in that manner. You should make sure that the tray has about 6 inches of depth and that the overall height of the cage is 15 inches as a minimum. Obviously, if you are going to go for a multi-level cage, you will want to make sure that the cage is much taller than 15 inches.

Ventilation in the cage is also very important and I recommend that you choose a cage with about bars set about ¼ to ½ an inch apart. This will ensure that your hedgehog can't escape his home while still providing ample ventilation for your pet.

If you are looking to build your own, avoid making the hedgehog cage with wood. Instead, use materials that can be cleaned easily. Plexiglas, metal and wire are great choices but you have to remember that ventilation is important when you do build the cage.

With flooring, you can choose to use something that is easy to clean and I usually recommend using a tile or a single piece of linoleum. Make sure that the hedgehog cannot pry it up or get his feet stuck between the pieces.

Setting up the Cage

Once you have purchased or built your cage, it is time to set it up. When you are doing this, it is important to note that African Pygmy Hedgehogs need a wide range of living areas and it is important to break the areas up into several different sections, which we will go over in this section.

The Bedroom

Yes, your hedgehog will need a bedroom and that is the first thing that we are going to look at when it comes to setting up your hedgehogs cage.

The bedroom is the area where your hedgehog will be sleeping during most of the day, remember, hedgehogs are nocturnal.

The first thing that you should do when you are creating the bedroom space is to create an area where the hedgehog can hide. In the wild, African Pygmy Hedgehogs prefer to sleep under leaves, in rock crevices or in a burrow. They love to be hidden away where they will be safe from predators.

Hedgehogs in captivity are no different and it is important to set up a place where your hedgehog can burrow under. The easiest solution to a house for your hedgehog is to purchase a tunnel/pet house that is designed for other larger rodents. You want to make sure there is room for an adult hedgehog, but usually a house built for a guinea pig is large enough.

If you want to make one yourself, you can use a host of different items such as:

- *PVC Pipe:* Take a pvc(acetate) pipe that is 4 inches in diameter and cut it into a 10 inch long piece.

Secure it onto one corner of the cage so it won't roll onto your hedgehog. Make sure that you sand the ends of the pipe to prevent your hedgehog from getting hurt on the sharp edges. PVC pipe is very easy to clean and your hedgehog will usually build a home at one end of the pipe.

- *Ice Cream Tubs:* A washed out ice-cream tub with a hole cut out of the side of the plastic, just large enough for your hedgehog is another great idea for a home. Like the pvc pipe, make sure that you sand the edges of the cut plastic to prevent injury.

- *Hedgie Bag:* You can purchase these but you can also make them easily with old fleece. Simple sew three sides of a folded square so you have a pouch that is about 10 to 11 inches in square. The hedgie bag can be placed inside one of the hedgehog's homes or left out for the hedgehog to snuggle into. If you use a hedgie bag, make sure that there are no loose stings or threads. Hedgehogs can get tangled in the threads very easily and can end up seriously injured.

You can also use things like old boots but whatever you use, make sure that it is easy to clean and that it won't present a health risk for your hedgehog if he chews it.

Lastly, make sure that the opening in your hedgehog home is large enough for the hedgehog to turn around in. The main reason for this is because hedgehogs prefer to exit and enter their burrows head first. If the burrow is too narrow, the hedgehog won't feel comfortable using his home.

Bedding

In addition to the proper home, hedgehogs require soft bedding to line their homes with. Most hedgehogs will bring the bedding into their burrows on their own; however, you will need to place it in the cage, close to the burrow so they will use it.

Over the years, there has been a lot of debate over what type of bedding to use for a hedgehog. Many people feel that cedar and pine shavings are fine for hedgehogs, however, over the years, there has been some evidence that these are harmful to hedgehogs. The main reason is that hedgehogs love to burrow into the bedding and both cedar and pine can have sharp splinters in the bedding, which has been linked to eye injuries in hedgehogs.

The other health concern is primarily towards cedar and the health problems for humans. Although the research is still being done, studies have linked cedar with an increase in asthma and glottal cancer in humans. Cedar shavings increases the amount of exposure to an aromatic toxin called Plicatic Acid, 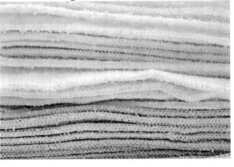 which is found in both cedar and pine, in a lesser amount, and it is not recommended that you use them for any small mammal pet.

Now that you know what to avoid for your hedgehog bedding, you should look for bedding that has a soft texture to it. In addition, it should be dust free to prevent irritating your hedgehog. Some examples of excellent bedding are:

- *Cloth:* Fabric bedding is one of the best choices that you can make for your hedgehog. Fleece, flannel and corduroy are the best choice. When you use cloth, make sure that there are no loose strings and avoid using a felt or anything that can be chewed apart easily.

- *Aspen Shavings:* If you want to use a shaving, use a chip aspen shaving. This is an excellent bedding for use with a hedgehog that has a skin allergy. It is very messy so be prepared for shavings outside the cage.

- *Paper Bedding:* There are many different paper beddings available and they are usually very safe for your hedgehog, although some brands can present a choking hazard if chewed. They are usually very easy to replace, however, it is important that you are aware that this is not usually a very comfortable bedding for your hedgehog and is not what I would usually recommend.

When you are selecting a bedding, you may have to play around with the different types until you find one that works for both you and your hedgehog. Make sure that whatever you choose, it can be cleaned easily or replaced on a regular basis.

The Exercise Space

Every hedgehog cage needs to have its own exercise space. A hedgehog that does not have space to exercise will quickly become bored and will start to have behavioural problems. In addition, a hedgehog that doesn't exercise will quickly become obese and this will shorten the lifespan of your hedgehog.

The exercise space does not have to be huge and you can provide exercise for your hedgehog out of the cage, which I will go over later on in this book.

The main item that you should have in this area is an exercise wheel. When you choose a wheel, there are a few things you should consider and these are:

1. *That it is a silent running wheel.* Remember, the most active time for your hedgehog will be during the night so for your own rest, make sure the wheel won't squeak. There are a number available at pet stores that fit this requirement.

2. *That it is solid.* Although the solid wheels are usually more expensive, it is better to go with this since the wired wheels can pose a safety risk for hedgehogs. The solid wheels will keep them from falling through the bars and hurting their legs. In addition, make sure there are no sidebars on the wheel since they can cause injury when the hedgehog looks out the side of the wheel.

3. *That it is the right size.* Make sure that it is about 12 inches in diameter. While wheels that are smaller will work for young hedgehogs, anything smaller than 12 inches will be too small for an adult hedgehog.

4. *That it is easy to clean.* Like anything you put in the cage, make sure that it is easy to clean.

5. ***That it fits your cage.*** Lastly, make sure that it fits your hedgehog's cage. If it is too big, it won't give your hedgehog enough room to really enjoy his cage.

In addition to the actual wheel, you should have a few pet safe toys that are designed for rabbits and guinea pigs. The more things your hedgehog has to do, the happier he will be.

The Bathroom

Not everyone provides a litter box for their hedgehog; however, I strongly recommend it. Hedgehogs can be litter trained, which I will go over later in this book and the best way to do it by giving them access to a litter pan.

When you are choosing a litter pan, make sure that it is easy to clean. Do not purchase anything that is porous, as it will only begin to smell after a few uses. I recommend a metal pan but if you use a plastic pan, make sure that it is a coated plastic.

With size, you would fit it to your cage, however, try to find one that is about 6 inches in length at the least but the ideal is a 12-inch square box. You also want to make sure that there is a 2-inch depth so that the hedgehog can get into the litter box easily but is able to cover the waste after he goes.

Litter boxes can be filled with a number of different types of litter, however, it is recommended that you avoid clumping or clay kitty litter since that can lead to health problems in your hedgehog due to the clay causing impaction. I recommend that you use a plant based litter or a paper based litter.

One point that you should take into consideration is that if you are using paper bedding, you should avoid using a paper litter as the hedgehog will have difficulty differentiating the two.

To keep your hedgehog's litter box fresh, use about 2 tablespoons of baking soda every time you clean the litter box. It will help keep the smell down on the box.

When you are setting up your cage, make sure that the litter box is as far from the food and water dishes as possible.

The Kitchen

The final area in your hedgehog cage should be a place where the hedgehog will eat his meals. As I mentioned in the last section, you will want to keep the area as far from the litter area as you can and if you are able to place it on different levels that is the ideal.

With the kitchen area, it is important that you are able to provide your hedgehog with two separate dishes for its food. Use heavier dishes that are about 2 inches in height. I recommend using a ceramic dish with a flat bottom, as the hedgehog won't be able to tip them over as easier as lighter, rounded bottom dishes.

Make sure that you have a dish for dry food that your hedgehog will be eating and that you also have a dish for wet food. With both dishes, they should be easy to clean.

In addition to the food dishes, you should have a water bottle for your hedgehog. Most rabbit water bottles will work for a hedgehog, however, before you use a water bottle, make sure your hedgehog was using one at the breeders.

If he wasn't, you will need to use a water dish at first, at the same time as using a water bottle. Eventually, your hedgehog will learn how to use the water bottle.

If you do use a water bottle, make sure that you always tap the bottle down so there is a drop of water in the actual dispenser.

If you prefer to use a water dish, make sure you clean the dish daily. In addition, elevate it slightly above the rest of the cage, using a stone tile, so not as much bedding gets into the water.

With the whole cage, place down linoleum or a cloth so the hedgehog has a comfortable floor plan. Make sure that you choose something that can be cleaned easily.

And that is all you need to do to set up your hedgehog's cage. While it may seem like a lot, there are actually only four different areas and they can take up very little room in the cage itself if you plan it properly.

Placing your Cage

In addition to the set up, it is important to understand the ideal place to put your cage. While it may not seem like a huge issue, setting up your hedgehog cage in the wrong area can lead to health problems and could shorten the lifespan of your hedgehog.

When you are placing the cage, there are a few things that you need to take into consideration.

Temperature

The best temperature for an African Pygmy Hedgehog is between 74° to 82°F. Some can do well with it being slightly warmer or slightly hotter but the closer to 74°F, the better your hedgehog will enjoy his home. Too cold and your hedgehog could become sick, too hot, and your hedgehog could succumb to heatstroke.

Although it may be easy to adjust your heating according to your own thermostat, some homes have too many temperature fluctuations to properly maintain a constant temperature for a hedgehog. To help with this, you can heat the cage artificially. The best choices are:

- *Electric Heating Pad:* This can be placed under the cage and you should make sure that none of it can be accessed by the hedgehog. Place it under the cage so that it covers half of the cage. It is important for your hedgehog to be able to move away from the heat.

- *Space Heaters:* A space heater can work well for hedgehogs as well but it is important to be aware of the safety concerning space heaters. Keep them away from the cage and anything that can is flammable. A space heater will heat the entire room so only use these if you are comfortable with a warmer space.

- *Heating Lamp:* You can purchase heating lamps from the pet store that are designed for lizards. Never use a heat lamp that has a plastic socket or use a heat bulb in a regular lamp. Heat lamps come in several watts but I recommend that you use a 100 to 150 watt bulb. Never use anything larger. Like the electric heating pad, you need to place it in the corner of the cage so the hedgehog can move away from the heat. In addition, place the heat lamp onto a timer so it will click off once a predetermined temperature has been reached.

Always be careful when you are using artificial sources of heating for your pet hedgehog. It is very easy to overheat them and while you may want a cooler cage, the cold will make your hedgehog slip into hibernation.

If you find that the cage gets too hot, specifically in the summer, you can cool the hedgehogs down by placing a frozen icepack on the top of the cage. Again, make sure you place it in a corner of the cage so the hedgehog can move away from the area if it gets too cold.

Remember to monitor the cage when you are cooling or heating it artificially to make sure that the temperature stays at the ideal or as close to the ideal of 74°F as possible.

Drafts

This ties into the temperature but make sure that your hedgehog's cage is not set up in front of any windows, vents or fans. Even on hot days, you should avoid pointing a fan at the cage as it can cause serious health problems for your hedgehog. Another area that you should avoid is close to an outer wall. Many times drafts can occur in this area and the outer wall is always the coldest in the room. Remember, this is an animal that needs a constant environment.

Lighting

Another important component of placing your hedgehog's cage is lighting. While many people feel that this animal needs low light, hedgehogs actually need at least 10 to 12 hours of indirect sunlight every day. If the light is too low, the hedgehog will hibernate and this could reduce the lifespan of hedgehog.

When you do set up the cage, make sure that the hedgehog will not receive direct light. It may seem beneficial to the animal, but hedgehogs can suffer from heat stroke very quickly so make sure to avoid this. Direct light will raise the temperature of cage very quickly.

If your hedgehog does not get good lighting in your space, use a daylight lamp with no more than 60watts. These lamps should be set on a timer and should run for the natural daylight hours, up to 14 hours. Do not leave them on all the time and make sure that it is set up in one corner of the cage so your hedgehog will not become overheated.

Traffic

The last thing that you should look at in regards to placing your hedgehog cage is the actual traffic that will be passing by the cage. While many hedgehogs can adapt to a busy household and do very well in a high traffic area, some can suffer from stress due to the traffic.

One thing that I recommend you do is slowly acclimatize your hedgehog to the high traffic. When you first bring him home, keep him in a quieter spot in the home. Once he adjusts to his new home, slowly move him into the high traffic area. Eventually, you can set up his permanent space in the high traffic area.

However, if you find that your hedgehog becomes stressed by the activity, place him in an area where there is light traffic.

Although it seems like a lot of information to consider for one cage, how you prepare for your African Pygmy Hedgehog will determine how happy and healthy the hedgehog will be in the future.

Once your cage is set up, you are ready to bring your hedgehog home, which we will go over in the next chapter.

Additional Equipment

Although the cage will be most of the equipment that you will need for your hedgehog, there are a few other things that you should consider having for your pet. These are:

Carrier:

Make sure that you have a hard sided carrier available for travelling with your hedgehog. Many can cope well going out with people but you want them to be secure. If you use a carrier, I would recommend getting a hedge bag for your hedgehog.

Toys:

Hedgehogs love to play so make sure you have a variety of toys. Some great toys are tunnels (you can use toilet paper rolls), cat toys, small balls and small rodent toys. Make sure that they are not too small, so that your hedgehog could swallow them.

Exercise Pen:

I always recommend that you either purchase or make your own exercise pen for your hedgehog. Although you may not realize it, hedgehogs are very active and can travel up to 1000 feet every night. This means that you should have space in addition to the hedgehog's cage.

If you prefer not to have an exercise pen, use an exercise ball for your pet so he has the ability to exercise outside of his cage. If you set up a cage, fill it with multiple items and make it so it can be changed up.

Hedgehogs love to climb so give him opportunities to climb by placing in branches, blocks and other climbing items. Make sure that they are not too high, as the hedgehog could fall.

In addition to climbing, place his toys into the exercise pen for different stimulation. You can also make his exercise pen into a maze with plastic dividers. Hedgehogs do very well with mazes and it is something I would recommend.

With the exercise pen itself, use a plastic bin that is high enough so the hedgehog can't climb out of it.

Wading Pool:

Hedgehogs often enjoy water so it is good to have a small plastic container that could serve as a wading pool for your hedgehog. Again, you want it to be large enough for your hedgehog to swim around and use the playpen. Make sure that the water is not too deep, where the hedgehog would drown. Always monitor your hedgehog when he is using his wading pool.

Grooming Supplies:

In addition to everything that I mentioned, it is important to have grooming supplies for your hedgehog. Some of the things you will need are:

- *Nail Clippers:* Baby nail clippers often work well for hedgehogs but you can purchase pet nail clippers.

- *Shampoo:* Always choose a vegetable based shampoo and avoid anything with fragrances or chemicals. In addition, do not use Tea tree oil products on your hedgehog as it can be toxic.

- *Oatmeal Bath Treatment:* This is only needed when your hedgehog has dry skin or is quilling.

- *Nail Brush:* A human nail brush is the perfect tool for scrubbing quills during a bath so I recommend picking some up.

- *Bag Balm:* A lotion that can be applied to dry skin.

As you can see, the list of items that you need for your hedgehog is quite large but in the end, if you have everything, your hedgehog will have a much happier and healthier life.

Chapter Six: Bringing your Hedgehog Home

You have your supplies, have picked out your hedgehog and now it is the time to bring your hedgehog home. While it may seem straight forward from this time on, bringing your hedgehog home should be done properly to ensure that you start out on the right foot.

In this chapter, I will go over everything that you need to do to successfully bring your hedgehog home from the breeders.

Age of a New Hedgehog

One thing that I should stress before you bring your hedgehog home is the actual age that you should do this. While some breeders and pet stores will sell them at a younger age, you should avoid bringing a hedgehog home before he is 6 weeks of age.

After 6 weeks, your hedgehog can come home but again, try to avoid purchasing an older hedgehog if you want the hedgehog to bond completely with you. That isn't to say that an older one won't, but it may not be as strong of a bond as it would be with a younger hedgehog.

The Carrying Case and Travelling

Although many stores will have a carrying case for small mammals, I recommend bringing your own, even if you are purchasing from a pet store. The main reason for this is so your hedgehog will have the least stress as possible.

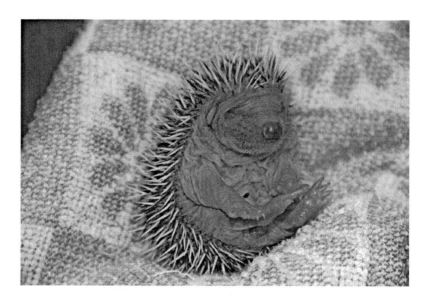

As you know, in the last chapter, I recommended purchasing a travel case for your hedgehog. Make sure that it is a solid cage and that there is no place where the hedgehog could slip out.

Before you travel to pick up your hedgehog, place some bedding into the cage. You want a large amount of bedding so the hedgehog can burrow down into the cage. You can also put in a hedge bag for your little one to snuggle into.

Remember that the move can be very stressful on a hedgehog so having plenty of bedding for the hedgehog to burrow down in will help prevent this.

When you do travel with your hedgehog, simply place him in the cage and allow him the chance to get comfortable.

Place the cage in a secure location in your car so it won't shift around. Do not place him in the trunk. Once he is in the car, leave him alone for the entire trip. Don't feel the need to comfort him as the hedgehog won't be able to get comfort from someone he hasn't bonded with.

If you travel for a long period, and plan to do a stopover, give the hedgehog some water along the way, place a dish in the carrier when you stop or use a water bottle through the whole trip. Also, offer the hedgehog food in a bowl but don't be worried if he doesn't eat. When he gets home, he will begin eating again.

At Home

When you arrive home, it is important to carefully transfer your hedgehog to his prepared cage. Never prepare the cage after you get your hedgehog home as this will only cause him stress.

Once he is home, you should place the hedgehog in his cage and leave him alone. Generally, I recommend that you do not interact with him for 12 hours at the very least. This will give the hedgehog time to become familiar with his space and will help reduce the amount of stress he feels from the transition.

When he is in isolation, avoid checking on him in the cage and simply stay away from it. In addition, do not try to pick him up while he is getting comfortable. It can be a difficult 12 hours for you but, trust me; the end result will be worth the wait.

Before you place the hedgehog into his isolation, make sure that you take the time to put fresh water into his cage. Remember, check with the breeder to find out how he has been receiving water. If it was from a bowl, use a bowl, if not, use a water bottle.

Also offer a wide variety of food to your hedgehog. It may seem like a bit much but the more variety you can offer him, the more likely he will eat during the transition. Although you will want to provide staple food, which I will go over later in this book, you should also offer snack foods that the hedgehog will be more tempted to eat.

Once the 12 hours are up, you can begin the process of bonding with your hedgehog. If you purchased the hedgehog from a reputable breeder, you should have a hedgehog that has been well socialized. This will make early handling easier since he will be more accustomed to handling.

Regardless, every hedgehog can have periods when they will huff or curl up, especially during the first few days at their new home. This is completely normal so don't become worried. Simply take the time to carefully pick him up and sit with him.

Don't over stimulate him during this period and make sure you only hold him close to the ground. Young hedgehogs, or hedgehogs that are in a new home, will often jump from hands and can easily be injured with falls.

For more on bonding with your hedgehog, read chapter nine: socializing your hedgehog.

The Vet Visit

Before you bring your hedgehog home, it is important to have a veterinarian chosen. While they do not receive all of the same care you would expect for a larger pet, they do require some care, which I will go over later in this book.

Having a vet before you bring him home, one that specializes in small pets, will ensure that your hedgehog is looked after in the case of an emergency.

Once your hedgehog is home, you should set up an appointment for your hedgehog about 14 days after he arrives. This is a wellness check up so the vet can determine if there are any health problems right away. In addition, it will get both your hedgehog and your vet used to each other.

Your Hedgehog's Temperament during the Move

Earlier in this book, I discussed the hedgehog temperament and while your hedgehog will probably grow to have this temperament, it is important to note that during the move your hedgehog will have a slightly different temperament.

For one, since your hedgehog is quite young, you will find that he is sleeping more than you expect. This is completely normal and will begin to adjust as your hedgehog ages.

In addition, during the first 24 to 48 hours, you will find that your hedgehog is not eating. Again, this is completely normal during a transition and should be expected. If your hedgehog does not eat after 48 hours, seek medical help for your hedgehog as something could be wrong.

Another thing you may see is the hedgehog not drinking. Again, this could be from the transition, but it could also be from the different taste in water. To help initiate water consumption, pour the water into a bowl and offer it that way. Often, the aeration through pouring changes the taste enough to get the hedgehog drinking.

Remember that your hedgehog is going to be a little off during the first few days or even weeks. He will be a little more vocal and will probably be very jumpy. This is completely normal and can be corrected by handling your hedgehog as much as possible.

In the end, your hedgehog will adjust to his new home and will quickly become the charming little creature you expect.

Chapter Seven: Caring for your Hedgehog

Your hedgehog is home and you are now settling into the day to day life with your beloved pet. Although I have mentioned that day to day care is not as involved with an African Pygmy Hedgehog as it is with other pets, there is still a significant amount of care that needs to be done.

Before we begin, I want to mention that this looks at daily care and not at the feeding or the handling of your hedgehog. Since feeding and handling is quite extensive, I have taken the time, later in this book, to look at them on their own. Handling is covered under Socialization and Training and feeding is covered under Feeding your Hedgehog.

Daily Care

After you look at feeding and handling, the daily care of your hedgehog is actually quite simple. It will only take a few minutes out of your schedule and then the remainder of your African Pygmy Hedgehog's care is simply enjoying time with him.

To start, it is better to group care into sections and in this chapter I will go over each section of daily care needed.

The Cage

Although we don't often think of the cage when we think of daily care, it is very important to take care of the cage on a daily basis. If you do, your hedgehog will have a clean place to live and will be less likely to have diseases or parasites.

In addition, a clean cage will help eliminate any smells that your hedgehog may have. On a daily basis, you will want to do the following in your hedgehog's cage.

- *Clean and wash the food and water dishes.* Make sure this is done daily, especially the moist food container.

- *Sift through the shavings.* If you have shavings, make sure that you sift through it and remove any spilled food or other debris. Dirty shavings can lead to many other problems, including foul odour.

- *Scoop the litter box.* Make sure that you scoop out the litter box on a daily basis. This will help cut down on the odour completely.

- *Clean toys.* Clean any toys that have been left in the hedgehog cage. You can also throw out any toys that your hedgehog seems to be bored with.

- *Fill the Water Bottles.* Make sure that you fill the water bottles on a daily basis so that your hedgehog has a constant supply of fresh water.

In addition to the daily cleaning, take the time once a week to wash down the entire cage and all the items in the cage with soap and water. Make sure that you use pet safe soap and cleansers when cleaning.

Change out any shavings and bedding that you are using in the cage as this will keep everything fresh and tidy. If you find that your litter box smells too strongly, replace the litter and sprinkle a small amount of baking soda into it.

Wash any fabrics as you need to.

And that is really all you need to do with the cage. There isn't a lot that needs to be done but the more you stay on task with keeping it tidy the less likely it is that you will have any noticeable odour coming from it.

The Hedgehog

On a daily basis, nothing major has to be done with the daily care. Make sure that you provide him with food and water daily and that you also give him a few treats every day. In addition, make sure that you handle him on a daily basis. It is better to handle him in the evening when he is at his happiest but if you find your schedule does not allow for that, handle him at an earlier time.

One last thing that I recommend that you do with your hedgehog is to check his weight on a regular basis. Hedgehogs that are over 1000 grams need to be monitored but it is not always a sign of obesity. When you are weighing your hedgehog, make sure that you check his chin and legs. If he has a double chin and the legs are very chubby, it is time to start reducing his food intake.

Exercise

Exercise is very important for a hedgehog for two reasons.

1. It helps eliminate boredom for the hedgehog.
2. It helps prevent obesity.

African Pygmy Hedgehogs will exercise on their own if you leave a wheel and some toys in the cage but it is important to offer them a variety of exercise. Bring your hedgehog out of his cage on a daily basis and allow him to play on the floor. You can also purchase a ball and have him run around on the ball if you are worried that he will get away.

In addition, create a playroom for your hedgehog with a plastic bin and allow him to explore the many different obstacles that you put in place. The more you mix it up, the more exercise your African Pygmy Hedgehog will enjoy.

It is important to note that you should give your hedgehog about a half hour of playtime and exercise time. You can use treats to keep him motivated or simply allow him to explore on his own. Make sure that you monitor him closely when he is not in his cage as he could be injured very easily.

Exercise Outdoors

Exercising outdoors is very similar to exercising indoors but it is something that you will only do parts of the year. In addition, it is not something that you need to do on a daily basis.

Before you allow your hedgehog to exercise outside, make sure that you are following these recommendations:

- Proper Temperature: Make sure that the temperature is between 74° to 82°F when you take him outside. If it is colder or hotter, you could make your hedgehog sick.
- Free of Pesticides: If you are letting your hedgehog crawl around on the grass, make sure it is free of any harmful pesticides.
- Safe from other Animals: Always let your African Pygmy Hedgehog exercise where there is no risk of other animals. In addition, make sure you steer clear of any areas where raccoons have been. The urine of a raccoon contains an illness that could kill your hedgehog.
- Access to Food and Water: Always take out food and water for your hedgehog when he is outside.

When you do take him outside, you can place him in a cage or bring out his cage so he is safe. One thing that I stress with this is to be aware of the weather since it can shift very quickly. Never leave your hedgehog outside for an entire day but you can usually leave him for an hour.

Always supervise your hedgehog when he is not in a secure cage outside but even when he is, check on him regularly to make sure that he is still fine.

Grooming

Although we often think of grooming as a daily task, for your African Pygmy Hedgehog it is not. You can groom your pet on a weekly or biweekly schedule; however, I do recommend that you keep an eye on him to make sure that he is always well groomed. If you find that he is dirty or his nails seem long, it is time for a grooming, regardless of how much time has passed since he was last groomed.

In this section of the book, I will go over all the areas where you will need to focus your grooming attention on.

Clipping Toenails

One of the more frequent grooming practice that you will do with your hedgehog is to clip his toenails. Although it may seem like a difficult thing to do, it is actually quite easy once you become familiar with it. Clip your African Pygmy Hedgehog's toenails whenever they look long.

1. Clean the hedgehog's feet with lukewarm water. Dry them completely before you begin clipping.

2. Place the hedgehog on a towel under good light. You will want to work up on a table for this task as it makes it much easier to see.

3. Take a paw in your hand. The best way to do this is to slide your hand under your hedgehog and then grasp the foot and turn it so you can see the nail.

4. Carefully place the clippers onto the nail. You should only clip the pale part of the nail and should avoid any part with a pink colour to it. This is the quick and it will bleed if you cut it.

5. Make a straight cut on the nail. Move to the next nail. It is important to note that hedgehogs wear down their nails naturally; however, it is never at the same rate so you won't have to clip every nail.

6. Move on to the other paws.

If you happen to cut the quick, place the nail is styptic powder immediately and it will stop the bleeding.

And that is all you need to know about clipping your hedgehog's nails.

Bathing your Hedgehog

Bathing your African Pygmy Hedgehog is something that should be done once or twice every month but I stress only bathing your hedgehog when he needs to be bathed. There are actually two different ways to bathe your hedgehog. Most of the time, you can simply give him the equivalent of a hedgehog sponge bath but if your hedgehog is really dirty you will need to give him a full bath. I will go over both in this section.

The Sponge Bath

With the sponge bath, you will need to have a toothbrush or nail brush, a small bowl of lukewarm water, tweezers and a towel.

1. Place your hedgehog on the towel on a flat surface where he won't fall. I recommend sitting on the floor with your hedgehog for safety.

2. Using the tweezers, pick out any large pieces of debris that is caught in his quills.

3. Once his quills are free of the large debris, dip your toothbrush in the lukewarm water.

4. Rub the quills, starting at the top of the hedgehog. Make sure that you do long strokes from the root of the quill and down the length to the point. Do not scrub in the opposite direction.

5. Rinse the toothbrush frequently, usually after each brush.

6. Pat the hedgehog dry.

7. Use a dry toothbrush to brush the quills once more and to also brush the fur.

The Full Bath

Washing a hedgehog in the sink is very similar to washing him with a sponge bath; the only difference is you are using running water. Make sure you pick out any large debris before you place your hedgehog in the water.

1. Plug your sink.

2. Place a towel into the sink so the hedgehog can rest on it safely.

3. Run lukewarm water into the sink until there is enough water for the hedgehog to be standing in half an inch of water.

4. Place your hedgehog in the water.

5. Using a cup, carefully pour water over your hedgehog. Try to avoid getting water in the ears and eyes.

6. Dip your toothbrush in the lukewarm water.

7. Rub the quills starting at the top of the hedgehog. Make sure that you do long strokes from the root of the quill and down the length to the point. Do not scrub in the opposite direction.

8. Rub the fur down with the toothbrush.

9. Make sure you rinse the toothbrush frequently, usually after each brush.

10. Rinse the hedgehog off with more water, which you pour onto him using a cup.

11. Remove the hedgehog from the water and place onto a dry towel.

12. Wrap the towel around him and then spend some time simply petting him with the towel. Make sure that your hedgehog is completely dry before placing him back in the cage.

No matter how you give him a bath, make sure that he is calm during the bath and that you keep it calming. If the hedgehog becomes frightened, simply stop the bath and spend some time soothing him.

When your hedgehog is young, give him more baths as this will get him better acquainted with bathing and less fearful of it.

Skin Care

Skin care is another area where you don't need to do a lot of extra steps with. You should take the time every day to check the condition of his skin and make sure that there are no parasites. In addition, make sure he has no cuts or injuries. If you see them, wash the cut carefully and to check it daily to make sure it does not become infected.

One of the main problems that you will find is dry skin. Hedgehogs can be prone to it so it is important to check it. The best way to combat dry skin is to place a few drops of mineral oil in the hedgehog's food every day. This will help keep the skin in good condition.

If you find the skin is dry, place a few drops of mineral oil directly onto the skin and allow it to coat the area. The hedgehog will clean itself when you do this but it should be enough to get the skin back to its normal health.

Dental Care

Dental Care is not something that you need to worry about too much. You will not need to brush your hedgehog's teeth, but again, try to keep an eye on your hedgehog's mouth as much as possible. If he seems to be having difficulty eating or has stopped eating, take him to the veterinarian.

Hedgehogs can have periodontal disease, which is a tooth and gum disease, so it is important to make sure that you provide your hedgehog with harder food, such as dry cat food. This will help work off any plaque and other dirt on his teeth.

Eyes and Ear Care

Ear and eye care is not something that you often have to worry about. There is not a lot of grooming and unless you have been prescribed drops by your veterinarian you can usually leave them be.

However, even though you are not fussing with them, I recommend that you do a regular health check on them when you groom your hedgehog. Make sure that there are no signs of parasites and that there is no debris in the ears or eyes. For the ears, check to see if there are any signs of tattered ears, which I will go over in the section on health.

To clean your African Pygmy Hedgehog's ears follow these steps:

1. Take the hedgehog gently into your hand.

2. Carefully hold him so you can gain access to his head without frightening him. This works much better with a hedgehog that has been handled a lot.

3. Dip a Q-tip into mineral oil. Squeeze out the excess oil so that the tip is damp but not dripping.

4. Swipe the outer edges of the ear carefully. It is better to come from below and to the side so the hedgehog does not become frightened.

5. Do not insert the Q-tip into the ear but just do the outside of the ear.

Only clean your hedgehog's ears when it is absolutely necessary.

With the eyes, simply wipe the hedgehog's face with a damp cloth if the eyes appear dusty. Also, make sure there is no damage to the eye. If you suspect damage, take your hedgehog to the vet.

And that is all it takes to properly care for a hedgehog. It may seem like a lot but generally you can spend only a few hours a week dealing with his daily needs. The rest of the time is spent simply enjoying your pet.

Chapter Eight: Feeding your Hedgehog

Understanding how to feed your hedgehog is a very important part of properly caring for your pet. If you provide a poor diet, you will find that your hedgehog has a poor quality of life and will also have more health problems, especially as he ages.

Before you begin to understand your pet hedgehog's diet, it is important to understand the wild hedgehog's diet. Although most people are aware that hedgehogs are insectivores, many people are not aware that hedgehogs are opportunistic feeders.

What this means is that they will eat anything that is available to them and it makes them more of an omnivore than an insectivore.

In the wild, hedgehogs will eat insects, small mammals such as baby mice, small lizards and amphibians and they will also eat fruit, roots and anything that is edible.

Although you will be feeding your hedgehog a planned diet, as opposed to an opportunistic diet, what this knowledge of wild hedgehog diets offers you is more variety for your hedgehog.

The Basic Hedgehog Diet

Okay, so your hedgehog's basic diet probably isn't going to be as diversified as the wild hedgehogs, but that doesn't mean that you can't offer your hedgehog a range of different foods.

When it comes to diets, there are a lot of different things that you can choose and it is important to provide your hedgehog with the proper nutrients. Remember that some foods can be considered snack foods and are not something you should feed in abundance to your hedgehog.

One thing that should be mentioned is that diet is a highly debatable topic in the hedgehog world. We are still learning about the proper diet for the pet hedgehog and while most of the information that is available is widely accepted, there is always new information being brought forward. For this reason, it is important for you to constantly update your knowledge on the latest information regarding hedgehog diet.

While there are many things that we don't know, we do know that hedgehogs require certain things in their diet. These are:

Protein:

It is very important for your hedgehog to have a diet that has a good source of high quality protein. In fact, up to 20% of the diet should be protein and it is often better to have a slightly higher protein level. If you are breeding your hedgehog, you will want a protein level of up to 35% of his daily intake.

With protein, it is important to use a high quality protein source. Although hedgehogs can eat foods that use pork and beef for their main sources of protein, chicken and lamb are better choices for a hedgehog. The main reason for this is that the latter are much easier for a hedgehog to digest.

In addition, it is much better to choose a food that has multiple protein sources as this provides a wider variety when it comes to nutrients.

When you are trying to find a staple food that has a high protein level, check the actual ingredients list and make sure that the first two ingredients are meat.

Fat:

Like protein, fat is an important part of health and growth, as long as there is a proper level of fatty foods. Generally, your hedgehog should receive between 5 to 15% of fat with his daily food intake. Make sure you choose the percentage according to your hedgehog. If the hedgehog is overweight, offer him a lower fat percentage and if it is underweight, offer a higher one. Young hedgehog babies and nursing females will need a higher amount.

Fibre:

Fibre is another important part of your hedgehog's diet so don't avoid foods with a good fibre content. On average, a hedgehog will need up to 15% of fibre in their daily diet. This fibre is often found in many foods but it is important to note that dry foods contain more fibre than moist foods. If you are feeding your hedgehog a wet diet, make sure you offer him additional fibre through a supplement.

Vitamins and Minerals:

With vitamins and minerals, most hedgehogs will get the proper amounts simply from the foods that you are giving them. However, some hedgehogs need additional supplements and it is important to purchase a hedgehog vitamin supplement if you decide to use one.

With vitamins and minerals, I recommend supplementing only when you have the following circumstances:

- Your hedgehog will be travelling.

- Your hedgehog is ill.

- Your hedgehog is under a year old.

- Your hedgehog is stressed.

- Your hedgehog is pregnant.

During the rest of the time, your hedgehog does not require additional vitamins and minerals.

When you are choosing a food for your hedgehog, it is important to remember that the hedgehog has a small mouth. Always use food that is small in size and make sure that you crush any larger kibbles that you use.

In addition, find a kibble that has a medium hardness to it. If it is too hard, the food could damage your hedgehog's teeth and if it is too soft, it could lead to tooth decay.

Types of Food

Now that you understand the importance of some nutrients in your hedgehog's diet, it is time to go over the types of food that you can give your hedgehog. Later in this chapter, I will go over treats and also food you should avoid, but for right now, let's focus on the staple foods.

Firstly, hedgehogs should have a varied diet and this should include both dry and moist food. Dry foods can be the following:

Hedgehog Food

Years ago, there was very little variety when it came to the staple foods. No company was producing a good hedgehog food but today more and more companies are producing one.

Generally, hedgehog foods are more expensive than other foods that you can offer your hedgehog and they can be more difficult to find. Many companies are online and the food needs to be delivered but if you can find it locally, I recommend using it.

When you are looking for a hedgehog food, make sure that it has the nutrients that I went over in the last section.

Cat Food

Cat food is a food that is often recommended for hedgehogs since it has a high level of protein. Over the years, people have used cat food as the primary food for their hedgehog and this is something that you can still do.

When you are choosing a cat food to use, make sure that it has a good protein level. In addition, choose one that uses chicken and lamb instead of seafood, beef or pork. Also look for one that has a low ash.

With cat food, you want to make sure that you choose a high quality cat food. Do not use a low cost store brand as this will only affect your hedgehog's health later in life.

Dog Food

Dog food is a food that I don't usually recommend. Usually, it is much too big for the hedgehog and needs to be crushed or moistened. Still, it has much of the same ingredients as cat food and many hedgehog owners have had success with this food.

Generally, my recommendation is to choose a high quality dry food that is either designed for cats or for hedgehogs. Avoid using dog food as it is simply too large for the hedgehog to eat safely.

Soft Foods

As I have mentioned, hedgehogs should have a combination of dry and moist food, although their primary diet should be dry. Moist food can be a range of items from canned cat or dog foods to cooked eggs.

It should be given in small quantities and should be given once a day. A good rule of thumb is about 1 teaspoon every day. When you are giving soft foods, take the opportunity to offer your hedgehog some variety. One day you can give the hedgehog cooked egg, the next cat food and the day after that some cooked poultry.

Since soft foods is not the main part of your hedgehog's diet, you can choose a variety of foods as long as they will not upset your hedgehog's stomach. Read the section on foods to avoid for more information.

Fruits and Vegetables

These can be grouped in with soft foods, but it is recommended that you offer your hedgehog the occasional fruit or vegetable. Generally, fruit and vegetables that are harder should be cooked to make them a soft food. Things like bananas and soft fleshed melons can be fed raw.

I recommend offering your hedgehog some type of fruit or vegetable every day, usually about ½ teaspoon of one type. It is important to note that hedgehogs are not herbivores and while some can grow to love fruit and vegetables, others will avoid eating them all together.

Do not worry if your hedgehog does not eat them but continue to offer them on a regular basis.

On a side note, hedgehogs cannot survive on a vegetarian diet, even if they enjoy eating fruits and vegetables, this is an insectivore and they need the nutrients derived from a meat based food.

Feeding your Hedgehog

Now that you understand what to feed your hedgehog, it is time to look at the fine points of feeding them. While some pets can simply have the food left out for them, hedgehogs require a bit more attention than that.

Before I look at when to feed your hedgehog, and how much to feed him, I want to stress that you should always monitor your hedgehog's food intake.

Make sure that he is eating but don't assume that he isn't getting enough if he eats everything in his dish. Hedgehogs are prone to overeating so it is important to weigh your hedgehog on a bi-yearly basis. If the hedgehog is gaining weight during the six months, after he has reached maturity at 6 months, then he is getting too much. If he is losing weight, then he is not getting enough.

Monitoring your hedgehog's food intake will ensure that you catch feeding problems early on before it becomes a problem.

Another point about feeding is that it is important to keep your hedgehog's dishes clean. This is very important with the soft food dishes since bacteria can grow on the dishes if they are not cleaned daily.

When to Feed

Since hedgehogs are a nocturnal animal, it is better to choose a time in the evening to feed your hedgehogs. Dry food can be placed in the cage and left in it all the time while soft food should only be put in during the evenings and then taken out after a few hours.

How much to Feed

How much to feed really depends on your individual hedgehog, however, I would recommend placing in about half a cup of dry kibble each day and then giving 1 teaspoon of wet and half a teaspoon of fruit or vegetables. After that point, you can offer your hedgehog treats throughout the week.

How to Feed

Many people are tempted to teach their hedgehog to eat food from hand but this is something you should avoid. Many hedgehogs will learn to bite simply because they are looking for food when you are handling them. Instead, always place food in the dishes.

When you are feeding treat, use a small set of feeding tongs or with a small dropper. This will give you the ability to feed your hedgehog "by hand" without running the risk of teaching your hedgehog to bite that hand.

Watering your Hedgehog

Watering your hedgehog is a very important aspect of caring for your pet. Hedgehogs need a constant supply of fresh water and you should have some in the cage, either in a bottle or in a bowl.

Every day, you should remove the water from the day before, clean the water container and then fill it with fresh water. It is important to note that many hedgehogs avoid tap water so you may have to purchase bottled water or filter your water to ensure that the hedgehog is getting enough.

If your hedgehog does not get enough water, he can begin to have kidney problems and this can result in premature death.

Treats for your Hedgehog

As I have mentioned already, treating your hedgehog is a very common thing to do and it is an excellent way to help with the bonding process.

Treating can be done in a variety of different ways and these include:

- *Stimulation:* Using them in mazes, hiding them in the cage, or simply placing them out of reach so the hedgehog has to problem solve will stimulate and enrich your hedgehog.

- *Foraging:* Wild hedgehogs love to forage and pet hedgehogs are no different. Placing treats around their cage will give your hedgehog things to do when you can't interact with him and will help alleviate his boredom.

- *Variety:* Providing treats for your hedgehog allows for the ability to really offer some variety to your hedgehog's diet.

- *Bonding:* As I already mentioned, treating your hedgehog when it is time for handling will make your hedgehog much more excited to be handled. Remember to use feeder tongs when you do treat during handling to prevent bites.

When you are giving treats, it is important to choose the right one. Later in this chapter, I will go over foods to avoid but some of the guidelines that you should consider are:

- *Food is the right size for your hedgehog.* Remember that hedgehogs have a small mouth so make sure the treats are small enough to be eaten without choking being a problem.

- *Keep treats small in quantity.* While it can be tempting to feed your hedgehog several treats, it can be very easy to fill up your hedgehog. Remember, treats are considered junk food so your hedgehog shouldn't use this food as his staple food.

- *Only use treats when regular feeding is successful.* Later in this chapter I will go over feeding problems, however, treating should never begin until your young hedgehog has established his feeding routine. In addition, if your hedgehog stops eating his staple food for any reason, treats should be taken away until you can get him eating again.

- *Go slow with the treats.* Make sure that you slowly introduce treats to your hedgehog and try to do it one at a time every few days. Mark down treats your hedgehog likes, treats he doesn't like and treats that seem to cause stomach or intestinal upset. This will help you find the perfect treats for your pets.

When it comes to treats themselves, there are actually a large number of treats you can offer your hedgehog. These are:

- *Insects:* Although insects are a staple food for wild hedgehogs, they should not be for your hedgehog. Instead, they should be a treat for your hedgehog. When you choose an insect, make sure they have been gut loaded or make sure to gut load them yourself, which means that they have been fed and are full of nutrients. In addition, never use large insects and never use superworms as they will bite your hedgehog and can be difficult to digest. Some excellent insects to feed your hedgehog are:
  - Freeze Dried Insects
  - Silk Worms
  - Crickets
  - Meal Worms
  - Wax Worms

- *Egg:* I have mentioned this several times but eggs are an excellent treat that is full of nutrition. Make sure that the egg is either hard boiled or scrambled and never feed the hedgehog raw egg.

- *Fruits and Vegetables:* I have already mentioned this as a daily food but you can also use it as a treat. Remember to only use soft fruit and vegetables or fully cook hard vegetables so they are soft. Never give the hedgehog hot food and make sure it is fully cooled before giving it to the hedgehogs. It is important to note that hedgehogs are not always interested in fruit or vegetables, so if your hedgehog prefers other treats don't worry. Some great fruit and vegetable treats to give your hedgehog are:
  - Bananas
  - Asparagus
  - Peas
  - Papaya

- o Watermelon
- o Green Beans
- o Blueberries
- o Strawberries
- o Apple
- o Radishes
- o Zucchini
- o Bell Peppers

- *Baby Food:* Another popular treat, baby food is usually a great choice and you can offer a wide variety of option with it. With baby food, avoid any with sugar or salt and make sure there is no garlic or onion powder in it. In addition, it is often a better option to go with an organic blend.

- *Meat:* Small pieces of cooked meat is another great choice for hedgehogs. Again, never feed your hedgehog raw meat and make sure that the meat is unseasoned. Lastly, make sure the meat is cooled completely before feeding it to your hedgehog.

- *Pet Treats:* Cat treats, rabbit treats, etc, are excellent treats as well. When you are using them, again, check to make sure that there are no ingredients that could be harmful to your hedgehog.

With treats, you really need to do a trial and error. Some hedgehogs love certain treats, others don't so don't be deterred if you have a difficult time finding the perfect treat. Eventually you will find it, and in the meantime, you can use his staple food as a treat to help with bonding.

Introducing New Foods

Whether you are introducing new staple food or new treats, there is a specific way that you should be introducing your hedgehog to new foods. Do not simply place in a variety of foods and expect your hedgehog to do well on them.

Instead, when you are introducing new food, it is important to introduce only one new food. Initially, your hedgehog

may not be interested in eating the food but you should continue to offer it until he does or until a week has passed and he has shown no interest.

If he does try the food, continue to offer it to him for about 3 to 4 days. Watch for any signs of stomach upset. If there are none, then the food is good for him and you should make note of it. If there is, then you should stop giving the food to your hedgehog.

After the food has been accepted, you can move onto the next food you want to introduce. It does take time but going slowly when you introduce new food will prevent a lot of problems.

One thing that should be mentioned is that some foods and some treats can change the stool that your hedgehog has. You do not have to stop giving the treat if it is a slight change but if it is a major change, then stop using that food in your hedgehog's diet.

Food to Avoid

As I have mentioned already, there are a number of unknowns about the hedgehog diet. We do know that they will eat whatever is available but even with this trait; experts have found that there are some foods that should not be eaten by a hedgehog.

Below is a list of foods that you should avoid feeding your hedgehog.

- *Avocado:* This is one of the foods that is often viewed as controversial. Some people say avocados are safe for hedgehogs, however, more and more evidence points to avocados being toxic to them. I tend to err on the side of caution so I recommend that you avoid them completely.

- *Dried Fruits and Vegetables:* Although this is often a treat for many small pets, hedgehogs have been known to choke on raisins and other small dried fruits and vegetables. Avoid using them. In addition, raisins and grapes can be toxic to some animals.

- *Raw Eggs:* Although eggs is listed as an acceptable treat for your hedgehog, you should avoid giving him raw eggs as they can lead to salmonella poisoning.

- *Chocolate:* Chocolate is toxic to many animals including hedgehogs.

- *Seeds and Nuts:* While it may seem tempting to give your hedgehog a seed or nut treat, avoid doing so. Like dried fruits and vegetables, seeds and nuts can present a choking hazard for your hedgehog.

- *Fried Foods:* Hopefully there is no temptation to offer your hedgehog fried foods but if there is, avoid it. Not only will fried foods make your hedgehog overweight, it can also upset your hedgehog's stomach.

- *Garlic:* Another food that is known to be toxic. Avoid feeding garlic and using foods that have garlic in the ingredient list.

- *Processed Meats:* While there will be meats in your hedgehog food that have been processed, you want to avoid any processed meat such as canned meats, deli meats and hot dogs. This does not provide any nutritional value to a hedgehog's diet and it can lead to stomach upset.

- *Raw Meat:* Like raw eggs, giving your hedgehog raw meat can increase the chance of salmonella poisoning.

- *Onions:* Onions are the same as garlic and they can be toxic to hedgehogs. Avoid using them and also avoid giving your hedgehog any food that has onions or onion powder in it.

- ***Milk and Milk Products:*** Never feed a hedgehog milk as they are known to be lactose intolerant. Milk can lead to severe stomach and intestinal upset in your hedgehog.

- ***Salty Food:*** Salt is not good for anyone and it is not good for a hedgehog. Avoid salt since it causes stomach upset and it can also lead to electrolyte imbalances, which affects the hedgehog's health.

- ***Wild Insects:*** Although it may seem like a cost effective way of feeding your hedgehog insects, you should never feed your hedgehog wild or outdoor insects. The main reason for this is that it can be very easy to choose one that is harmful to your hedgehog. The second reason is that wild insects can have parasites that will make your hedgehog very sick.

Since your hedgehog may not be very picky when it comes to food, it is important for you to be picky for him. Avoid these foods and your hedgehog will thrive on the diet you are giving him.

As you can see, there is a lot of information on diet but it is important to follow it thoroughly. Again, always update on the information about hedgehog diets and follow through on the changes you need to make.

It may seem like feeding a hedgehog is hard but once you choose the diet you want to work with, it becomes very easy to provide a high quality diet to your pet.

Feeding Problems

The last thing that I would like to go over in this chapter is the feeding problems that you can encounter when you are feeding your hedgehog.

There are actually several different problems that you can face and I have included a few tips to overcome them.

Picky Eating

Hedgehogs can be notoriously picky when it comes to food. Some hedgehogs will get into a food jag, which is where they will only eat one type of food for an extended period.

They will often have some favourites and will turn their nose up at anything else that is offered to them. To overcome picky eating it is better to start young. Make sure you offer them plenty of variety when they are younger and they will be more accepting of new food when they are adults.

In addition, whenever you offer a new food, you should try to offer it in many different ways. Hand feeding, placing it in the cage for foraging, using it as a stimulation. The more variety you use when introducing, the better chance you will have of getting your hedgehog to eat the new food.

Lastly, make sure that you stick with it. The more you offer a new food to a hedgehog, the more likely he will try it. As I mentioned in introducing new foods, give it a good week before giving up on the new food.

Hunger Strikes

A hunger strike is where a hedgehog will stop eating and often drinking and while not every hedgehog owner will see a hunger strike, they are quite common.

In fact, they often occur when there is a change for the hedgehog. This could be a change in the food, a move of the cage, or even a fluctuation in temperature. In addition, illnesses can lead to hunger strikes so it can be difficult to determine what is causing your hedgehog to stop eating.

If your hedgehog does have a hunger strike, one of the very first things you need to do is eliminate the cause. Make sure that your hedgehog is not sick or injured. If you think he is, take him to the vets.

If it is due to an environmental change, focus on getting your hedgehog to start eating. Generally, when a hedgehog is having a hunger strike, offering him a soft food will get him eating faster than sticking to dry kibble.

Once he is eating small bites of soft food, such as canned cat food, start mixing the regular kibble with the cat food.

It can take a bit of time and perseverance but if you keep offering your hedgehog his favourite foods, eventually he will begin to eat again. If you need to, you can use a can of Ensure, baby formula, and force feed your hedgehog with an oral syringe but usually# they will eat on their own after a few days.

If he does not begin eating after three to four days, it is important to seek medical help as there may be additional problems that are causing the hunger strike.

Obesity

I have mentioned obesity several times but it is a problem that many hedgehog owners are faced with. It can be difficult to determine how much food your hedgehog is eating so it is very important to monitor his weight.

If you find that your hedgehog is becoming obese, it is time to put him on a diet. Reduce the amount of protein and fat that he is getting. You may have to change his regular dry food to do this.

In addition, cut down on the treats and make him exercise for the treats. It can take a bit of time to get him back to his fit self but once he is there, you can re-establish his regular diet but make sure you make some changes to it to avoid significant weight gain again.

As you can see, feeding your hedgehog can be a challenge but once you get over a few of the teething troubles surrounding it, you should be able to offer your hedgehog a rich and varied diet.

Chapter Nine: Socializing and Training your Hedgehog

Socializing your hedgehog is a very important part of properly caring for and raising your hedgehog. If you purchased the hedgehog from a reputable breeder, then socializing will have already begun.

If you haven't, then you may have a slightly harder time with socializing but with patience every hedgehog can become a very sociable pet. In this chapter, I will go over everything you need to know to make your hedgehog as charming as possible.

The First Few Weeks

If you have not read the chapter on bringing your hedgehog home, I strongly recommend that you read it. In that chapter, I went over the first few days that your hedgehog is at home with you.

To recap, it is very important to let the hedgehog be by himself for about 12 hours after he comes home. After that time, you can begin to pick him up but make sure that you do not fuss at him. Hedgehogs enjoy being handled but it is important to be calm, especially during the first few weeks that he is home.

When you begin approaching your hedgehog, it is very important that you simply place your hand calmly near where he is. Let him get used to your smell. At the beginning, you will probably find that he moves away from you when you come close, but after a few times he will begin to move forward and sniff your hand.

Do not try to pick him up or touch him when he does, simply allow him to sniff you and then move along on his way. Once he sniffs you and moves away, slowly remove your hand.

If you want to get your smell associated with comfort, place a t-shirt or blanket into the cage that has your scent on it. If you use it as bedding for the hedgehog, he will begin to see you as a safe place.

Make sure that whatever you put into the cage is hedgehog friendly and that there are no loose strings that could wrap around the hedgehog's limbs.

Once you have spent some time getting your hedgehog used to your scent, you can begin handling him. With handling, I recommend that you try to pick him up every half hour when he is alert. The more he is handled, the faster he will bond with you and be accepting of being handled.

With the first greetings over, the first few weeks after that point should be spent with the hedgehog simply sitting on your lap while you engage in another quiet activity.

Do not sit and pet it but simply place your hand in your lap and allow him to sniff around your hand and move into it if he chooses too. You want to sit down on the floor so if he does bolt, he won't fall and become injured.

Again, do this for several days. While it may not be active interaction, it is passive interaction and will enable the bond to grow.
As he becomes more familiar with you, you can begin to pick him up and handle him.

With touching your hedgehog during those first few weeks, always start off by touching his back end first. Never touch his face before you have successfully handled him and he is comfortable with you.

As he becomes more accustomed to you, gradually move up his body until you can touch his back and sides, and then finally move up to his head. Take it very slowly and expect it to take several weeks to be allowed near his face.

In addition, during those first few weeks, allow your hedgehog to snuggle into you and hide if he is scared. This is actually a very good thing and it will teach him to go to you for comfort if he becomes frightened.

Remember to always start slowly and to put your hedgehog down if you find that he is becoming stressed. Don't worry; your hedgehog will get there eventually.

Picking up a Hedgehog

Although I have already talked about socializing your hedgehog in those first few weeks, it is important to know how to pick up a hedgehog. Many first time hedgehog owners make the mistake of picking up a hedgehog incorrectly and this often results in a minor injury.

Before you pick up a hedgehog, I strongly emphasise that you should always use your bare hands. The only time I recommend using gloves is when your hedgehog is sick and/or injured or when you are trying to administer medication.

The rest of the time, you should use your bare hands as this is less threatening to a hedgehog and will also help speed up the bonding process with your hedgehog.

One thing that should be pointed out is that handling a hedgehog does not hurt. In fact, the quills of a hedgehog are not very sharp and they lack barbs. What this means is that while the quills may sting slightly, they will not do significant damage to your hand.

When you go to pick up a hedgehog, it is important to come at the hedgehog from the sides. Do not come at him from the top or from the front since this will startle him and will cause him to pop, which is when he curls up into a ball.

Instead, place your hands on either side of the hedgehog at the back of him. Slowly bring your hands forward and in. Carefully slide your hands under the hedgehog and lift him.

If you go calmly, then your hedgehog should be fine. Once you are holding him, take him to an area where he won't be injured if he falls.

Occasionally, even a fully socialized hedgehog will pop when you are going to pick him up. If this happens, simply rock him gently in your hands. Eventually, he will relax and unroll. Don't put him away as this will just create a problem with handling.

If you find that doesn't work, rest the hedgehog in one hand, head facing away from you and massage near his neck. Do this gently and eventually the hedgehog will poke his head out. When he does, stop massaging and simply allow him to crawl into your other hand if that is what he would like to do.

Hedgehogs and Children

Hedgehogs can do very well with children; however, it is important for you to teach the children how to hold the hedgehog. Make sure that you always have the children hold the hedgehog on the ground and that you also have them remain quiet and calm when holding the hedgehog.

One thing that should be mentioned is that African Pygmy Hedgehogs tend to bond with the person who handles him the most and will usually avoid other people. If it is your child's pet, make sure that the child takes the time to be the primary caregiver and handler. It is a lot of work so make sure your child is old enough to take responsibility.

Hedgehogs and Pets

Hedgehogs and other pets should not mix so it is important to keep them separate. Remember that hedgehogs can trigger a prey drive reaction from other pets so it is best to keep them separate.

While hedgehogs can be very affectionate to their primary caregivers, they are a solitary animal and are happy to be on their own.

Hedgehog Social Behaviours

This could be placed throughout this book but since it is linked to the social interaction with your hedgehog, it is important to look at it in this section. As I have mentioned throughout this book, hedgehogs have a wide range of behaviours that will endear them to you. Some are sweet but some behaviour can be shocking when you first experience it. For this reason, I will go over everything you need to know about their behaviour.

Curling Up

As you know, hedgehogs will curl cup so that their quills will protrude in a criss-cross pattern. The rolled ball looks very similar to a sea urchin and is a big deterrent to predators.

Hedgehogs usually curl up when they are feeling frightened and you will see more curling in the early stages of socialization. Once a hedgehog bonds with their owner, they are less likely to ball up. One thing to mention is that a hedgehog will usually give a sign that he is about to curl up. This is through huffing and snorting so if you hear these sounds, avoid picking your hedgehog up.

Vocalization

Hedgehogs are actually very vocal and many times, their different sounds can identify how they are feeling. It is very important to understand your hedgehog's vocalization so you know when to interact with the hedgehog and when to leave him alone.

- *Singing:* This is only seen when you are breeding your hedgehogs. It is a very strange sound and usually has a number of squeaks and chirps in a sequence.

- *Chirping:* Again, associated with breeding, chirping is the noise of young hoglets and is usually the first sign that there is a new litter.

- *Squealing:* A sign of injury so make sure you monitor your hedgehog. If you place two hedgehogs together it is often a sign of a fight.

- *Huffing:* This is a huff sound, almost like the hedgehog is panting. It is a sound telling you to leave the hedgehog alone.

- *Sneezing:* Sneezing can be a sign of illness but it is also used in other ways. Some hedgehogs use sneezing when they are being curious, others use it when they want space. You need to understand how your hedgehog uses sneezing before you decide how to react to it.

- *Clicking:* A clicking noise is a sign that your hedgehog is being aggressive.

- *Purring:* This is a happy sound and one all hedgehog owners love to hear. It is a sound that says your hedgehog is content.

- *Grunting:* Like purring, grunting is a sound of happiness and contentment.

- *Popping:* Similar to clicking, it is used for either aggressive purposes or when your hedgehog is defending itself or young.

- *Hissing:* Hissing is another sign of protection or aggression.

- *Screaming:* It is always associated with a severe fear or with a severe pain. Check your hedgehog if you hear screaming and contact your vet if you think something is wrong. One thing that should be noted is some hedgehogs will occasionally scream in their sleep for no apparent reason.

- *Whistling:* Finally, whistling is a cute little sign of contentment.

Self Anointing

Self anointing is a strange little habit that all hedgehogs will do. This is when they will experience an object and will begin to chew on it. Once they are finished chewing, they will create a foamy saliva. This saliva is then wiped over their body so that they will smell like whatever they have been chewing.

It is behaviour that scientists have not been able to find a purpose for. Some believe it may be a way to camouflage their scent, others believe that it may be a way to rub toxins on their body for defence. Most hedgehog owners find that self anointing happens when the hedgehog finds something interesting.

If you see your hedgehog self anointing, simply allow him to do so, although you may have to give him more baths to combat the smell if the object that holds his interest is strong smelling.

Burrowing

As I have mentioned throughout this book, African Pygmy Hedgehogs love to burrow and they will do so in their cage or even when they are out of their cage.

In addition, hedgehogs will often burrow into their owner's clothes, especially when they are nervous. If your hedgehog is burrowing against you, simply comfort it and allow it to. It will only help build your bond.

Biting

Hedgehogs can bite, although they are not known as a problem biter. It is important to be aware of this habit and to avoid doing things that trigger it. One thing to avoid is feeding your hedgehog by hand. Always use feeder tongs so your hedgehog will not bite at your hand when he wants food or treats.

Outside of learned biting, hedgehogs may bite when they are scared or threatened. Make sure that you watch for signs that your hedgehog is under stress. This will help cut down on the amount of biting that occurs.

In addition, some hedgehogs will bite to express their emotions. Again, this is usually done when they are frustrated so be sure to understand your hedgehog's moods and temperament.

Scratching

Although scratching can be a sign that your hedgehog has a health problem, it is also a habit that they have. Many hedgehogs will scratch themselves when they are nervous and others will scratch themselves when they wake up.

If you see your hedgehog scratching, just keep an eye out to make sure that he does not have any parasites or dry skin but other than that, you can ignore it.

Training your Hedgehog

While a hedgehog will not learn like a dog will learn, they are actually quite clever and through the use of food you can teach a hedgehog to go over obstacles and through mazes. Really, there is no limit to the amount of fun you can have with mazes and your hedgehog as long as it is safe for your pet.

There are a few areas where you can train or condition your hedgehog.

Shifting Night to Day

Shifting your hedgehog's sleeping patterns is something that can be done but I recommend that you avoid doing so. Hedgehogs are nocturnal animals and while you may want them to be up during the day, shifting their schedule can greatly affect their temperament and health.

If you do plan on shifting their schedule, you will need artificial lighting for your hedgehog. Place the lights on a timer so that you have daylight during the night. This will cause the hedgehog to burrow and to sleep during the night while you are sleeping.

During the day, you will need to either have the hedgehog in a room that remains dark during the night or you will need to cover the cage with a dark blanket. Make sure that there is still ventilation so that the cage does not get too hot or you could hurt your hedgehog.

Your hedgehog will be awake during the day and will do all of his exercising during that time. When you arrive home, he will still be alert and you can spend more time with him without needing to wake him.

Again, I stress that you only do this if you feel it is absolutely necessary for your hedgehog's health and happiness.

Litter Training

As you know, hedgehogs can be litter trained but it is important to note that simply placing a litter box into the cage won't mean your hedgehog will go in that box. In addition, if you let your hedgehog wander free in your home, you will need to put in some effort to make sure he is going in the right place.

Start by placing a litter box in the area where you want it to be.

Sequester your hedgehog to the area. If you are letting him out in the house, make sure that his first few days are spent in the room with the litter box. If you have him in the cage, partition off the other sections of the cage so he needs to stay close to the litter box.

Make sure you give him access to a bedding area as you do not want your hedgehog to be left solely in the litter box.

Leave him be while he is litter training. Watch him to make sure that he is going into the litter box, but if he isn't, move the litter box to the location he is going. The majority of hedgehogs prefer to go in one spot and they will return to it repeatedly. If he has marked out a different area for eliminating, all you will need to do is move the box to that area and he will begin using the box.

Watch the hedgehog and if he has been using the litter box successfully for 3 or 4 days, open up the rest of the house or cage to him. Once a hedgehog is litter trained, he will remain litter trained.

Hedgehogs are a wonderful pet and as I have gone over in this chapter, the real joy of owning one is through the socialization and training.

Chapter Ten: Hedgehog Health

Before we begin a chapter on hedgehog health, it is important to understand that African Pygmy Hedgehogs are considered to be very hearty animals. They have very few health problems and with proper care, maintenance and diet, your hedgehog should maintain his health throughout his life.

That being said, there are times when health problems can occur with your hedgehog. For this reason, it is very important to understand the signs of illness, what can cause illnesses, how to administer medication and lastly some of the diseases that have been seen in domesticated African Pygmy Hedgehogs.

In this chapter, I will go over everything you need to know about these things but before I do, I want to stress the importance of having a qualified vet. As I mentioned earlier in this book, make sure that you have taken the time to find a vet who specializes in small mammals. It is better if they have experience with hedgehogs themselves, but if you can't find one in your area, find one that has worked with guinea pigs, rabbits and other small mammals.

Also, before any medical emergency care occurs, make sure that you take your hedgehog to the vet for a visit. This will help with socializing your hedgehog to this situation and will give your veterinarian time to become familiar with a hedgehog.

The recommended schedule for taking a hedgehog to the vet is every 6 months. At this time, the vet should weigh your hedgehog and check his overall health. Generally, there are no vaccinations that need to be given and the visits are usually just routine health checks.

Signs of Illness

Before you look at the health of your hedgehog, it is important to understand the signs that your hedgehog is ill. I recommend that you do a regular, daily health check on your hedgehog every time you take him out of his cage.

Signs of an illness in a hedgehog are:

- *Listlessness:* The hedgehog is lethargic and does not appear to move often or very quickly.

- *Dull Eyes:* Eyes that are not shiny and bright are a sign that the hedgehog is ill.

- *Difficulty Breathing:* If the hedgehog is gasping for breath and seems to have a very hard time drawing it.

- *Rapid Breathing:* Like difficult breathing, if the hedgehog appears to be panting and does not appear to be hot.

- *Loss of Appetite:* Often one of the first signs hedgehog owners notice, a loss of appetite could be from an illness.

- *Limping:* Any signs of limping could be an indicator of an injury.

- *Bloating:* Bloating can be a bit difficult to determine but if your hedgehog's stomach is swollen and hard, there is a good sign that the stomach is bloated.

- *Sudden Weight Loss:* Hedgehogs that have a sudden loss of weight may be ill.

- *Vomiting:* I go over vomiting later in this chapter but any time your hedgehog vomits, you should monitor him to make sure you do not see further evidence of an illness.

- *Stool Changes:* If you see changes in your hedgehog's bowel movements, then there is an indication that there is something wrong. This can be constipation, which could be a blockage, or diarrhoea, which could be caused from food.

- *Unexplained Discharge:* If you see unexplained discharge from the mouth, nose, ears or genital areas, seek the help and advice of your vet.

Medical Problems

Although hedgehogs are a very hearty pet, they do experience some health problems and it is important for hedgehog owners to be aware of them.

Cancer

Cancer is an increasing problem in domesticated hedgehogs, including the African Pygmy Hedgehog. There are several types of cancers that hedgehogs can have and most of them start as a tumour under the skin but it has been seen in every part of a hedgehog, including internally.

Treatment for cancer varies depending on the type of cancer and the location of the cancer. It can include medication, surgery or even chemotherapy.

Wobbly Hedgehog Syndrome

Wobbly Hedgehog Syndrome is a nutritional disease that is actually known as Hepatic Lipidosis, or fatty liver. This is where fat cells begin to replace healthy liver cells and it reduces the function of the hedgehog's liver. The disease is often linked to toxic waste build up in the blood and is linked to obesity in your hedgehog or a low exercise level.

Symptoms of Wobbly Hedgehog Syndrome are very similar to Multiple Sclerosis in humans. There is an uncontrolled shaking as well as seizures. Eventually, the hedgehog will become paralyzed, starting in the back legs until it moves into the front legs.

The disease is a degenerative disease that is usually seen when a hedgehog is between 18 to 24 months of age. There is no known cure and usually the disease will take the life of the hedgehog within 6 weeks to 18 months after the first symptoms are seen.

There are no cures for this disease; however, medication is used to treat the symptoms of the condition and to improve the quality of life for the hedgehog.

Quill Loss

Quill loss is when your hedgehog will begin to lose his quills for no apparent reason. This could be due to a parasite or it could be due to a number of health reasons. If your hedgehog is over the age of 6 months and is losing his quills, take him to the veterinarian to determine the cause of the quill loss.

Mites

Mites are a very common parasite that hedgehogs can have and you may find that your hedgehog baby has mites when you bring him home. While it may not seem like a big deal, mites are extremely serious.

They cause many different problems for the hedgehog including flaky skin and quill loss. In addition, mites can cause blindness and can even result in the death of a hedgehog. If you see your hedgehog scratching, you should check to see if it has mites.

To do this, place your hedgehog on a dark, or black, cloth. Rub his quills gently and then remove the hedgehog from the cloth. Carefully place the cloth under a bright light and look for small white flakes that are moving. It is very difficult to see the flakes as an actual bug unless you have a magnifying glass.

If there are mites, take your hedgehog to the vet and use the treatment that he recommends. Before you place your hedgehog back into his cage, carefully disinfect everything that is in it. If there are wood products, remove them and throw them away.

Do the same with any place the hedgehog plays frequently. Continue to monitor your hedgehog for several weeks and retreat the space and hedgehog if needed.

Ear Infections

Ear infections can be seen in hedgehogs and they are often an indication that the hedgehog has mites or a nutritional imbalance. When you are checking your hedgehog, make sure you look for any sign of an infection.

The most common sign is a discharge from the ear. If you see this, make sure that you contact your vet immediately. Treatment is usually through a medication prescribed by the vet but it is important to keep the ears dry and clean even when an ear infection is not present.

Ear Fungus

Ear fungus is one of the leading causes of ear infections in African Pygmy Hedgehogs and it is usually picked up from the wood products that you place in a hedgehog cage.

While you may not notice the fungus in the early stages, you will begin to see the ears of the hedgehog becoming tattered and looking as though there are fingers around the edge of the ear. If you see this, then the hedgehog may have ear fungus and it must be medically treated. Leaving ear fungus untreated will lead to the ears being completely eaten away by the fungus.

Green Stools

Green stools is not really a medical problem but it is something that really concerns a new hedgehog owner when they first see it. The main reason for green stools can be a change in diet. Other reasons for green stools can be stress or changes in the hedgehog's environment.

Usually, if you see green stools, you do not have to do anything. You can check their diet to make sure that there is nothing giving them an upset stomach but don't feel you need to. Another thing to do is reduce the amount of stress your hedgehog is under, if that is possible.

If you are patient, your hedgehog's stools will change back to the proper colour after a few days. If they do not, and if they are loose as well, contact your vet to have him looked over. On rare occasions, green stools can be an indicator of a serious illness.

Dry Skin

Another common ailment in hedgehogs is dry skin. Again, this can be caused by a number of parasites and/or illnesses and it can also be caused by the lack of a high quality diet.

In addition, winter can dry a hedgehog's skin out and will lead to a dry flaky skin that is extremely itchy to the hedgehog.

When you see your hedgehog itching, take the time to make sure that there is no underlying cause for the dry skin. If there isn't, you can simply treat the skin by giving your hedgehog oatmeal baths.

In addition, adding omega fats to the diet will help with dry skin. You can use an omega fatty acids supplement but make sure that it is safe for the consumption of your hedgehog.

Another cure for dry skin is to place a few drops of Vitamin E oil on the hedgehog every day.

If there is an underlying problem or you suspect one, contact your vet to have it treated.

Allergies

Hedgehogs have allergies like all other pets and it can be difficult to determine what the root cause of it is. Generally, allergies are seen in the skin and the hedgehog may have dry, itchy skin.

If you suspect an allergy, look at your hedgehog's diet. If nothing seems new in the diet, check the supplies you are using in the cage. It can take a bit of time but if you narrow down the cause  of the allergy, you can alleviate many of the problems that are associated with them.

Before I close on the topic of health problems, I want to stress that many of the health problems that your hedgehog can have are zoological. What this means is that it can be transferred from the animal to humans so it is important to always wash your hands after handling a hedgehog.

In addition, children should not handle a hedgehog if you suspect that it is ill. Being careful with hygiene will help you avoid getting the illness yourself.

Administering Medication

Now that you know of the medical problems that your hedgehog can face, it is important to know how to properly administer the treatment for those illnesses.

Unlike many other pets, giving medication to a hedgehog can be a tricky endeavour. On the one hand, you need to be able to get the hedgehog to take the medication. On the other, you want to avoid the hedgehog from popping in your hand.

Before you give any medication, I recommend that you put on a pair of thick gloves. If the hedgehog does startle, you can avoid most of the quills with a good pair of gloves.

Oral Medication

Oral medication is one of the easier medications to administer since you can simply hide the medicine in a treat. The reason why I say treat is because you don't want the hedgehog to become turned off of his regular food if he doesn't like the taste of the medicine. In addition, putting it in regular food can make it difficult to determine if the hedgehog received the full dose.

When you mix the medicine into the food, use a soft food and mix one part of medicine to two parts of the food. Treat the hedgehog as you would normally.

And that is all it takes to administer oral medication to your hedgehog.

Injected Medication

Injected medication is a bit trickier than oral medication and this is when you may startle your hedgehog enough to make him pop or curl up into a ball.

Generally, hedgehogs do very well with injections but occasionally, they may startle.

Start by placing your hedgehog in your hand. Although you may feel that you need to inject the medication into the leg or belly, you do not need to do that. There is ample space for you to inject any medication and I recommend speaking with your veterinarian to determine the best place for your hedgehog.

Once he is in your hand, carefully place in the syringe and then release the plunger. Remove quickly. If the hedgehog does pop, avoid placing the syringe in and simply wait for him to relax to start again.

Dropper Medication

Dropper medications are another type of medication where the hedgehog may pop and again you will need to wait until the hedgehog calms down before you try administering it again.

With droppers, I recommend that you simply allow the hedgehog to stand naturally in an area that you can access him and that he feels comfortable in. When he is standing still, simply bring the dropper over the area that you have to administer the medication to.

If it is in the air, bring it from the side and then up. If it is the eye, bring it from the front. Never go directly above the hedgehog as this will make him pop.

Apply the medication as close to the site as possible. If you need to, you may have to handle him to administer the medication. Try not to glob the medication onto the area as that will give your hedgehog the opportunity to lick the medication and it could be dangerous if ingested.

Although it may seem difficult to administer medication to your hedgehog, if you have properly socialized your hedgehog, he will usually take medication very painlessly.

First Aid for your Hedgehog

It is every new hedgehog owner's hope that they will never have to rush their hedgehog to the emergency vet, unfortunately, accidents and emergencies do happen so it is important to understand how to deal with them.

How you administer to an injury or an emergency will greatly affect the outcome for your hedgehog. It is very important that you have a first aid kit in your home that is specially designed for your hedgehog. What you should have in your kit are:

- Cotton Swabs

- Sharp Scissors

- Heating Pad or Hot Water Bottles

- Cornstarch

- Antibiotic Cream

- Tweezers

- Oral Syringes

- Hydrogen Peroxide

- Gauze

- Medical Tape

- Iodine

Once you have your first aid kit, you are prepared to deal with some of the problems you may face. Below are a number of first aid techniques you can use with your hedgehog.

Transporting an Injured Hedgehog

While this may not be a first aid technique exactly, knowing how to properly transport a sick hedgehog is very important to ensure that he is successfully cared for.

Firstly, always place the hedgehog into a secure carrier. Make sure that there are blankets or a hedge bag in the carrier for your hedgehog to burrow into. Remember that you want to reduce the stress of travelling, especially if the hedgehog is sick or injured.

In addition to placing blankets into the carrier, make sure that you place a hot water bottle under the blankets. This will help reduce the shock your hedgehog may be feeling and will also help prevent a chill.

Remember to try to keep your hedgehog out of the cold as much as possible during transportation so that his temperature will stay regular.

Extreme Body Temperatures

As I have mentioned earlier in this book, it is very common for hedgehogs to either be too cold or too hot. Heat stroke from being in a warm space or in direct sunlight is very common, as is hypothermia when the temperature drops to a dangerously low temperature.

If you find that your hedgehog is suffering from hypothermia, place a warm heating pad under the cage or place a hot water bottle next to the hedgehog. Wrap the hedgehog in a towel and monitor. If he starts to move around and seems fine then you can simply loosen the towel and allow him to move from the heat source as he would like.

If you find that after two hours, your hedgehog is still listless, then it is time to seek medical help.

With overheating, place a frozen water bottle into the cage or on top of the cage and allow the cage to cool off. Again, monitor your hedgehog and if after an hour he shows no signs of getting better, take him to your vet.

Bleeding

Occasionally, a hedgehog can suffer an injury that can cause bleeding. When you see the bleeding, you should determine if it needs medical attention or not. Some small injuries can be given first aid at home without any adverse side effects for the hedgehog.

With a small cut, take a clean cloth and apply it directly to the injury site. Press down firmly until the blood begins to slow or until it stops completely. It may be better to put on thick gloves when you are going this as your hedgehog may bite simply because it is injured.

Once the bleeding stops, clean out the wound with hydrogen peroxide. Make sure you clean the area around the injury as well. Apply a small amount of cornstarch to the wound as this will help stop the bleeding completely.

After that point, monitor the injury and if you spot any signs of infection, contact your veterinarian. As the injury is healing, apply antibiotic cream to the injury site.

For larger wounds, it is important to seek medical attention. Before you take your hedgehog to the vet, however, stop the bleeding if it is possible in the same manner as you would with a minor injury. Apply pressure until the blood flow slows.

Once it slows, place gauze over the wound and tape it down with medical tape. If it is in a spot that is difficult to tape, you can place a tube sock over the bandage so that it moves from the front to the back of the hedgehog and presses the gauze and quills down onto the wound.

Depending on the injury, you may see blood on the face. If this is the case, seek immediate medical care but do not do any first aid. If it is coming from the mouth, inside the ears or the eyes, it could indicate internal injuries and the hedgehog must be seen by a vet. Any first aid is simply getting your hedgehog ready for transporting as outlined already in this chapter.

Bloody Feet

Although bloody feet is bleeding, it is treated slightly differently than major bleeding would be done. Generally, bloody feet occur due to minor cuts on the hedgehog's feet. This could be an actual cut or the nail being broken.

When you see your hedgehog with bloody feet, don't panic, simply wash the feet with warm water and apply antibiotic cream as it is needed.

After you have administered to the feet, try to find the cause of the cuts and, if possible, remove the hazard from your hedgehog's cage.

Shock

Shock is another problem that owners can be faced with for a number of reasons. Hedgehogs will often go into shock for many reasons but some common reasons are:

- Bleeding injury
- Fall
- Liver Failure
- Heat Stroke
- Dehydration
- Illness
- Stress

When you suspect that your hedgehog is in shock, carefully transport him to the vet. If it is due to dropping the hedgehog or a fall, carefully cut out a piece of cardboard. This should be a firm piece so that it does not bend under the hedgehog.

Secure your hedgehog to the cardboard with medical tape very carefully. You do not want to injure him further when you place him on the board.

Once he is on the board, place him in his carrier with a hot water bottle wrapped in a towel. Make sure that the hot water bottle can't shift onto your hedgehog and crush him.

Wrap the hedgehog in towels and make sure that he is as secure as possible in the carrier. Carefully transport him to the vets.

Vomiting

Vomiting is not a very common occurrence with hedgehogs but it can happen. Whenever your hedgehog vomits, make sure that you monitor your hedgehog for the next few days. If the vomiting becomes severe, contact your veterinarian and also collect the vomit in a small plastic bag for the vet to examine.

Once it is collected, store it for until you get to the vets. Generally, you can store it up to six hours before the sample is worthless.

After you have collected the vomit, monitor your hedgehog. If he seems fine, continue to watch him to see if he vomits again. If he doesn't, don't feel that you need to go to the vets. If he does, take him immediately.

While you are monitoring him, check to see if he is dehydrated at all. To determine this, pull a small section of quills up. If you find that the quills do not go back into place immediately, then your hedgehog is dehydrated. Dehydration is one of the biggest problems that you will experience when your hedgehog is vomiting and needs to be corrected as soon as possible.

If this is the case, feed him paediatric oral electrolyte solution in a dropper. Make sure that it is warmed slightly but not hot. Give him about half a teaspoon at a time, every half hour to an hour.

Diarrhoea

Diarrhoea is treated in much the same way as you would treat vomiting. Watch your hedgehog while he has diarrhoea and if it appears to be getting worse, contact your veterinarian.

Again, it is important to collect a sample if the hedgehog has severe diarrhoea as this will allow the doctor to determine if there is something affecting the hedgehog.

Before you contact your vet, however, it is important to look at your hedgehog's diet. Have you given your hedgehog a new type of food? If the answer is yes, simply remove that food from your hedgehog's diet. Monitor the hedgehog still but usually when you see diarrhoea after introducing a new food, it is the new food that is the culprit.

As with vomiting, you want to make sure that your hedgehog is not dehydrated from the diarrhoea. To determine this, pull a small section of quills up. If you find that the quills do not go back into place immediately, then your hedgehog is dehydrated.

If this is the case, feed him paediatric oral electrolyte solution in a dropper. Make sure that it is warmed slightly but not hot. Give him about half a teaspoon at a time, every half hour to an hour.

Constipation

Constipation is not usually very serious, unless it is accompanied with other symptoms or has been ongoing for several days.

To help alleviate constipation, feed your hedgehog a small amount of unseasoned canned pumpkin. If that does not work, place your hedgehog into a small pool filled with a few inches of warm water.

If the constipation lasts for a few days or nothing you do to correct the problem works, contact your vet.

And that is about all of the medical emergencies that you will see. There are other, more extreme problems that can occur such as a broken limp, however, if you suspect any type of serious injury or illness, it is best to securely place him in his carrier and take him to your vet.

Chapter Eleven: Breeding your Hedgehogs

Although you may not have purchased your first hedgehog with the intention of breeding, many new hedgehog owners quickly fall in love with these charming animals. This love quickly develops into a lifelong desire to continue adding to the domesticated lines of hedgehogs and breeding takes off from there.

If you are interested in breeding your African Pygmy Hedgehog, then it is very important to understand what you are getting into. While hedgehogs can be amazing parents, raising hedgehogs is not easy.

Firstly, breeding hedgehogs require specific care throughout breeding and into nursing the hoglets, or baby hedgehogs. Secondly, a female hedgehog will develop some changes to her personality, which can be difficult to deal with. Thirdly, if hedgehogs feel threatened or there is a shift in their environment they will kill their own young. What this means for you is that you could go through a lot of work, only to lose your hoglets during the first few days.

Raising hedgehogs is difficult and socialization, which I will go over later in this chapter, is quite demanding during those six to eight weeks when the hedgehog is with you.

The reason why I am focusing on the negative aspects of raising hedgehog babies is to emphasise that raising hedgehogs is not for everyone. You need to be dedicated and ready for any circumstance with breeding, including the negative ones.

With that aside, breeding hedgehogs can be a very rewarding experience and in this chapter I will go over everything you need to know to successfully breed and raise your hedgehogs.

Choosing your Breeding Hedgehogs

The very first thing that you should do is choose your hedgehog for breeding. Although any hedgehog over the age of 8 weeks can be bred, you should never choose to breed a hedgehog simply because you can. Some diseases are hereditary so it is important to find the healthiest hedgehogs.

With both the male and female hedgehog, it is important to look for these traits:

- *Free of Disease:* Never breed any hedgehog that has signs or symptoms of a disease. In addition, make sure that they do not have a history of diseases in their family. If they do, make sure that you avoid using those hedgehogs for breeding as they could, potentially, pass those diseases down to their young.

- *Sound in Temperament:* Although socialization will do a lot to producing a wonderful hedgehog, starting with parents that have an even and sweet personality will improve the odds that these temperaments will pass on to the young. Never breed a hedgehog that has an aggressive temperament or any negative temperament traits, no matter how beautiful they are. If you do, you could wind up with a litter of ill-tempered hedgehogs.

- *Conformation:* Along with temperament, you want to find two hedgehogs that have the looks and confirmation that you are looking for. Make sure that they have healthy quills, which is indicated by good colour, and that they are a strong and healthy specimen. Match the parents well so that the beauty of the young will be apparent at a very young age.

- *Proper Age:* The last thing that you should look at is the age of the hedgehogs. In general, you want them to be about 5 months of age before you breed them. With males, any time after 5 months is fine for them to breed for the first time; however, they should never be bred after 3 years of age. For females, you should always make sure that the first breeding takes place between 5 to 12 months. If you wait until after she turns one year of age to breed her for the first time, there is a high chance that she will not conceive. For hedgehog females, you should never breed them after they turn three years of age.

Once you have selected the hedgehogs you want to breed, you are ready to start breeding.

Breeding your Hedgehogs

The very first thing that you should realize is that hedgehogs do not have a set time when they can breed. When they are 8 weeks of age, hedgehogs can be successfully bred, although you do want to wait until they are much older.

After 8 weeks of age, a hedgehog can produce several litters of hoglets every year and some can produce up to 7 or 8, although this is not healthy for a female hedgehog. The maximum number of litters a female hedgehog should have is 2 per year. Anymore and you will greatly diminish her quality of life.

With breeding, it is very important for you to prepare for breeding. Start by cleaning the cage where breeding will occur. Generally, breeding should be done in the male's cage as placing the male into the females could cause problems between the two and may result in an unsuccessful breeding.

In addition, placing them in a new cage could lead to other problems since the hedgehogs may experience shock from being moved.

As I mentioned, it is very important to clean the entire cage to prevent disease. In addition, remove large obstacles that could hinder breeding. Toys, tubes, ladders – the main idea is to keep the hedgehogs on the same level so they cannot get away from each other.

Once the cage is prepared, place the female hedgehog into the male's cage. Leave them but make sure you monitor them from a distance.

One thing that I should mention is that mating and courtship can appear like something is wrong between the two. There is often a lot of noise and there can be some aggressive behaviour. If the hedgehogs are just making a lot of noise, then everything is fine, but if it becomes very violent with the hedgehogs causing physical damage to each other, then you should remove the female.

Generally, though, the male will often begin the noise in the cage by making plaintive squeaks. These are loud squeals that he makes as he chases the female around the cage.

His advances may be very aggressive in appearance but in general he will simply be following her around the cage.

The female will usually react in a different manner. Often, females will resist the advances of the male and will hiss, spit and will also physically attack him, although it won't be a violently enough to physically harm the male. After some time, the female will eventually give in to the advances of the male.

When this occurs, the female will flatten down on to the ground and will push her rump out towards him. Her quills will flatten down and she will appear submissive to him. At this point, the male will mount the female and mate with her.

Generally, courtship can take several days so it is recommended that you leave the male and female together for 7 to 9 days. It is also very important that you allow the hedgehogs to have some privacy during this period. While some will have no problem breeding in front of you, many will not mate if a human is watching.

After seven days, you can remove the female from the male's cage and allow her time to rest after being bred. One thing that is recommended is to return the hedgehog a week later and allow them to be together for another 7 days. This isn't always necessary but if a pregnancy did not occur during the first pairing, it is sure to take place during the second.

Birthing Hoglets

Now that your hedgehog has been bred, it is time to remove her from the male and set her up in her own cage. Never, and I stress never, leave a male and female hedgehog together when she will be giving birth. The main reason for this is it is not uncommon for parent hedgehogs to eat their young, especially if there is a male in the cage.

For your own records, I strongly recommend that you mark the dates of breeding on a calendar. If you are unsure of the

exact date when breeding occurred, mark the date of first breeding as the first day that she seems to accept the male.

From that date, you should expect the hoglets to be born approximately 34 to 36 days after that date. It is important to note that African Pygmy Hedgehogs can vary in gestation time. Some go as early as 30 days after the first breeding and some can be as late as 46 days. Make sure that you do not assume she is not pregnant if she does not give birth in this time frame as you may have dates off. In fact, you should give 11 days extra from the last possible expected due date, especially if you did a second week of breeding.

Although hedgehogs are happy to find their own space in their cage, it is important to give her a nesting box. I recommend using a 1 gallon, plastic ice cream pail. Cut the hole about 1 inch below the top of the pail so the hedgehog can easily get in and out but her young won't be able to wander out.

Once it is cut, fill it with bedding, place the lid on the pail and then turn it upside down. Place it in the cage for a week or two weeks prior to her first estimated delivery date so she has time to become accustomed to it.

After that point, leave her alone as much as possible. The more you fuss over her, the more stress she will have. The more stress, and the greater the chance of her eating her young.

As you are waiting for your hedgehog to give birth, make sure that you keep cleaning the cage on a regular basis. I recommend every two to three days so you are not fussing with her too much. The rest of the time, simply leave her alone and only check in from time to time to make sure that she is okay.

Do not take her out during the last week before her first due date for socialization as this can cause unnecessary stress for her.
Generally, hedgehogs deliver on their own and you should avoid interfering. Instead, watch for the day when she misses a meal. If she does, listen for soft chirps coming

from the nesting box. If you hear them, simply leave her alone.

Raising Hoglets

Once your hoglets arrive, there really isn't a lot for you to do during the first few days. Two weeks before her first delivery date, increase her food by about a teaspoon to a tablespoon. Keep the cage clean and then let the mom handle the rest.

During the delivery, the female hedgehog will do everything and she will also take care of the hoglets during the first few weeks. When hoglets are born, their quills are covered with a membrane. After 6 to 12 hours, the membrane will dry and the quills will begin to poke through. It is important to note that the first quills on a hedgehog are soft and almost resemble hair. At two weeks of age, the hard quills will begin to grow and the baby will begin to resemble his parents at that time.

Although some hedgehogs can have 8 to 9 hoglets, it is more common for them to have between 2 to 5 hoglets. They are born blind and will usually be about one inch long. Although it can be very tempting to check on the hoglets as soon as you hear the chirps, refrain from doing so. Instead, mark the date that you heard the first chirps and then leave them alone for 3 to 4 days.

Make sure that you still offer your female hedgehog that extra food and also make sure that you give her a larger quantity of food.

After the 4 days have passed, carefully look into the nest. Don't move nesting materials around to get a look at the hedgehog as you may inadvertently touch the hoglet. If you do touch a hoglet, the female may reject it or kill it. The first time you look in, don't do so for a long time, as the female will hiss at you to protect her young and you do not want to cause too much stress to her.

Make sure that you check on her on a daily basis after that initial visit. If you need to move a hoglet for any reason, use a spoon and scoop the hoglet up. This will prevent your scent from getting on the hoglet and causing problems with the mother. Don't be upset if a usually friendly hedgehog is hissing and being aggressive to you when you are checking her babies. This is simply a sign that she is a dedicated mother.

During the first three weeks, the hoglets will be kept in the nest and will feed solely on the mother's milk. There is no need for you to do any more than simply keep the cage clean and tidy.

Once they reach three weeks of age, the hoglets are at an age where you can begin to handle them. At this time, they should be opening their eyes and will be mobile. They may even be venturing out of the nest occasionally, but usually never too far.

It is very important, if you plan to properly socialize your hedgehogs, to handle them at this stage. It can be a bit scary at first as the hedgehog mother will begin to hiss and jump when you reach for her young. Again, this is completely normal so don't worry. Instead, pick her up and move her to a different spot in the cage where you won't be bothering her too much.

Pick up the first hoglet and place them into your hand and then allow them to uncurl on their own. This should only take about a minute or two minutes. Once they unroll, carefully place the hoglet into the nest and pick up the next hoglet.

With the first contact with the hoglets, make it very quick, no more than 2 minutes at a time. Slowly increase the time over the next two weeks. When they reach 5 weeks of age, you should take the effort to hold them for at least a half hour several times a day. Remember, the more you handle them, the better socialized they will be for your buyers.

When they start becoming mobile at 3 weeks of age, you can begin to introduce food to the hoglets. They will not be eating a lot of new food at first but by 5 weeks of age they should be eating on their own. Offer them the same diet that you offer the female hedgehog. In addition, make sure that you offer them water. Young hoglets may have a difficult time using a dropper watering bottle so you may have to use a bowl. If you do use a bowl, be sure to clean it several times during the day.

At six weeks of age, your hoglets should be completely weaned from the mother. There is nothing that you need to do except offer them an adult diet – the mother will do the rest.

When they are weaned, remove them from the mother's cage and place them in a separate cage. You can keep them together at this time but only for two weeks. Remember to handle your hedgehogs on a regular basis to ensure that they have ample socialization.

Give them an adult diet and start introducing treats slowly; please read the chapter on feeding your hedgehog for more on diet and nutrition.

At 8 weeks of age, sex the hedgehogs to determine the gender of each hoglet. To do this, place the hedgehog in your hand and turn him over so his belly is showing. Hold his tail out of the way if you need to but try to avoid handling him too much or he may roll up into himself. Directly under the tail, you should see a space between the genitals and the rectum. If it looks like there is a belly button in that space, which is created by a large gap there, then it is a male hedgehog. If there is no gap and the genitals are close to the rectum, then it is a female.

Separate all of the males and females. You do not need to use separate cages for each hedgehog at this age but you should have one cage for males and one cage for females.

In addition, at 8 weeks of age, your hedgehogs can begin to go to their new homes. It is important to note that hoglets will begin to grow their adult quills at 10 weeks of age. This is known as quilling and while some will remain the same colour, most will change to a different colour when their adult quills come in.

Raising hoglets is actually quite easy and all it really takes is the time and dedication to properly socialize them.

Fostering a Hoglet

As I have already mentioned, occasionally, hedgehogs will reject their hoglets. Although it is not uncommon for them to reject one or two hoglets in a litter, it is also not uncommon for them to reject an entire litter. If this occurs for you, be prepared for a lot of effort for your hoglets. Remember, these are babies and they will require plenty of attention during their first few weeks.

The very first thing that you should do when a hoglet or a litter of hoglets are rejected is to remove them from the cage. You should never leave them in the cage as that could result in the mother killing her own young.

Once you move them, set up a feeding schedule. Hoglets should be fed every 3 to 4 hours during those first three weeks. As they get older, you can reduce the number of feedings once they are introduced to solid food, but before that time, it is very important to feed them frequently.

To feed them, offer them kitten formula or goats milk. You can purchase kitten formula at most pet stores. Offer it to them with a dropper or a bottle that is designed for small animals.

Once you feed the baby, take a wet cloth and wipe the genital area. This will help the baby go to the bathroom.

Again, the main focus is on the feeding. Follow the same socialization schedule that you would if the mother was raising the hoglets herself. It is important to note that raising hoglets by hand will not guarantee a more socialized hoglet.

In addition, you should only hand raise hoglets if there are no other options to you. If you find that you need to raise them, I recommend trying to give them to another hedgehog. Place the rejected hedgehogs into the nest, making sure that you do not touch the hoglet as this will put your scent on them and cause the foster hedgehog to reject the young as well.

Fostering is much more successful when another hedgehog takes over the fostering. Generally, hoglets that are raised by hand have a very high mortality rate and most will die within a few weeks.

It is for these reasons that it is important to simply leave the mother alone during those first three weeks so she will be less likely to reject her young.

Chapter Twelve: Common Terms

So you are interested in owning a hedgehog. Well if you want to be a true hedgehog lover and owner it is important to understand a few of the common hedgehog terms that you will hear the moment you enter the hedgehog raising world. Below is a list of terms and words that you will experience in the hedgehog world.

Afterbirth: The tissue that is delivered after the birth of a sow's piglets. It includes the placenta and fetal membranes.

Carrier: A small and secure cage that is used for transporting a hedgehog.

Carnivore: An animal that eats meat as its primary food source.

Colostrum: A milk that is high in antibodies that is produced during the first few days after the baby hedgehogs are born.

Estrus: Part of the reproductive cycle, this is when the female is most receptive to males.

Foraging: A natural behaviour where the hedgehog will dig and push around items to get at food.

Gestation: The period of time that pregnancy takes.

Heat Lamp: A lamp that uses an infrared bulb, which produces heat.

Hedgehog: A small mammal that is considered to be an insectivore. It is identified by the short quills on its back.

Herbivore: An animal that primarily eats vegetation and plants as its main food source.

Hoglet: A baby hedgehog.

Inbreeding: Mating closely related hedgehogs

Insectivore: An animal that eats insects as its main food source.

Lactation: When milk is produced in a female that is nursing or about to give birth.

Line Breeding: Breeding two hedgehogs that are related through the same family line but are not as closely related as hedgehogs that are used for inbreeding.

Litter: A group of babies born from the same mother and father during the same period. Litters of hedgehogs average between 4 to 6 babies.

Nocturnal: An animal that is active primarily at night.

Omnivore: An animal that eats both plants and meat.

Ovulation: When the ova are released during the estrus period of reproductive cycle.

Popping: When the hedgehog startles and rolls into a protective ball.

Quill: The hollow spines that cover the majority of a hedgehog's body.

Quilling: The period when the hedgehog's quills fall out; usually occurs between 8 weeks and 6 months.

Sex: To determine the gender of the bird.

Standing Heat: A stage of estrus when the female hedgehog will allow a male to mount her.

Ventilation: To circulate air through a space to provide fresh air to that space.

Vulva: Female genitalia

Zoological: A disease or illness that can be transmitted from an animal to a human or vice versa.

Photo Credits:

2/13-B
8|13 W

CPSIA information can be obtained at www.ICGtesting.com
Printed in the USA
LVOW101503290113

317738LV00020B/1316/P